YOU ARE NOT ALONE
MENTAL HEALTH MENTORS –
TAKE THE JOURNEY WITH YOU

BY:
DOUG LAWRENCE

SILVER DAWN PUBLISHING

EST. 2019

DEDICATION

This book is dedicated to my wife, Debra, who lost her battle with cancer on February 6th, 2021. Part of her story is contained in this book as she had to live with my mental health challenges. She saw in me what others did not and it was her mission to bring back the Doug that she had fallen in love with.

I want to dedicate this book to Catherine Saykaly-Stevens who has been my mentor on my journey to write this book. She kept the fire burning when it was about to go out. I am forever Grateful for her support and friendship.

Finally, I want to dedicate this book to all those who have had a battle with mental health challenges. For those who have won that battle, congratulations! For those who have not been successful in their battle, I am truly sorry, and I extend my sympathies to your loved ones as they struggle with your loss.

FOREWORD

It's been a number of years since Doug and I first met. He called and introduced himself and wanted to meet to talk about his focus on mentoring. Since that initial meeting, we get together every so often to share the highs and lows of life. When Doug asked me to write the foreword for his book, I was taken aback and also honoured. As a consultant, trainer and author I have supported hundreds of individuals as they seek to focus on where they want life to take them whether that is in building their life, their career or their business.

Doug's book makes me think of all the mentors I have had in my life. They have helped me immensely! Guidance with my life, as a parent and as a business leader has helped me be the person I am today and Doug takes all that help and puts it together nicely here and then wraps a bow around it.

Doug isn't merely speaking platitudes about mentoring. He lives it! He shares his own story of his struggles with the traumatic situations he encountered as a member of the RCMP. As we can all imagine, life affected his mental health and he shares with us his climb out of the abyss.

Mental health is the key as he so masterfully explains. Without the support to keep a positive focus our mental health can cause us damage. His gift to us all is basically three-fold... to listen without interruption as the individual shares his or her story. And, as part of the listening element to hear what the individual is actually saying – as indicated, that takes listening to a whole new level. And finally, once you have the understanding of what you actually heard, then to speak asking questions to help the individual process and find new direction for themselves.

Having that closet door opened for you where you can see your life more objectively is critical. And often we cannot d that for ourselves. We simply need someone to hold our hand, let us know it is okay to ask for help and be accepted for who we are. After all, we all want to be accepted! It's okay to seek help, and if it is not available from one individual to go on to seeking help from someone else.

Are you available when someone comes to you for support? Such an important question that Doug mentions to help us realize our ability to support others. Too busy, too much work, not qualified... these are just some of the excuses one might express when asked for help. Don't! Everyone today, as Doug so carefully indicates, needs support in one form or another. Some are deep, some moderate and others pretty light. It doesn't matter – be there!

If you are a leader in your organization this book will hopefully give you some insights into what your employees are experiencing. If it doesn't, I would suggest you go back and read the book again. People today; your employees or their families and acquaintances (and yours too) are all struggling. Yes, some to a lesser degree than others, yet this world today has so many people with mental health struggles and that impacts the bottom line of business. So, do indeed, listen!

If you have picked up this book it is because you have a struggle. Read it, cover to cover, so you understand how you might help yourself or someone else through the challenges of the 21st century.

Doug has done an amazing job here with statistics, real life examples and support processes that can help everyone. Enjoy the journey – some of your family, friends and business co-workers are counting on you.

Sherry Knight, CPHR, FCMC, BA
President & CEO Dimension 11
Author of UnstoppABLE – 7 Steps to Living Your Personal Best

TABLE OF CONTENTS:

1. DON'T GO ON THIS JOURNEY ALONE

The doctor of the future will give no medication, but will interest his patients in the care of the human frame, diet and in the cause and prevention of disease.
—Thomas A. Edison

When I first started the journey of writing this book—one of two that I am working on—I reflected back on my previous book, The Gift of Mentoring (2014). I wanted to recreate the ambience of the two of us sitting side by side on a bench, and me sharing some stories of my experiences over the years. That feeling of settling into a long conversation with a good friend is the most important outcome for me. I won't make any promises as to what you should expect, but I encourage you to pick up a copy of this book and read it with an open mind. I've learned a lot while researching and writing this book, and I hope you will too.

I wrote this book to provide a solution to the increasing demand for mental health support. I believe, and my research shows, that there is a key part missing from most people's support structures in today's world. That key that can help people thrive and meet their challenges is mentorship. I believe that a mentor with mental health training would be of incredible value as part of a well-rounded mental health plan.

In this book, there's more than just research and facts. I've also included interviews with people who have either experienced mental health challenges, or who are supporting those that are battling with mental health issues. Their stories are very impactful and will give you a way to make a personal, empathetic connection with the idea of mentorship. As you go through this book, I want you to listen for the tools, tips, and techniques that I share, as well as those that you can identify in the interviews and case studies that I've shared. Each case study presents a particular problem for you to consider, and then some possible solutions to help guide you in addressing those situations. As always, I welcome your thoughts and comments.

I want you to come away from reading this book with some strategies and tools that you can use, both as a mentor and as a person seeking support from a mentor. I hope to show you how mentoring can become an integral part of your mental health support structure. My ultimate goal is to increase that pool of support structure personnel through the "gift of mentoring."

2. WHAT ARE THE SIGNS AND SYMPTOMS OF MENTAL ILLNESS IN THE WORKPLACE?

Mental health problems are a pandemic—a silent pandemic—and it is continuing to grow as the clock ticks on. According to the World Health Organization, "close to 800,000 people die due to suicide every year, which is one person every 40 seconds."[1] Those who commit suicide struggle with many problems, among them a failing support structure for mental health, few if any supports for mental well-being, and issues such as Post-Traumatic Stress (PTS). In fact, the WHO notes, "one in four people will be affected by mental or neurological disorders at some point in their lives."[2] As a result, the WHO estimates, "approximately 450 million people currently suffer from such conditions" which places "mental disorders among the leading causes of ill-health and disability worldwide."[3]

Anyone is susceptible to any or all of these illnesses. Sadly, the stigma that goes with these illnesses often prevents people from seeking help and they end up living a life of suffering. As the WHO's report shows:

Treatments are available, but nearly two-thirds of people with a known mental disorder never seek help from a health professional. Stigma, discrimination and neglect prevent care and treatment from reaching people with mental disorders. Where there is neglect, there is little or no understanding. Where there is no understanding, there is neglect.4

Mental illness can impact any of us, at any time in our lives. This is not something that is limited to a specific geographical location. It is a global issue and one that is not being addressed.

I will give an example of my own struggles to show how widespread these challenges can be. I am a retired Royal Canadian Mounted Police officer; I served for twenty-five years. I saw many traumatic things over that time period and I did not have a support structure in place to deal with that trauma. The organization did not provide the support structure that its members needed to address mental health. For example, I saw serious injuries where death was imminent, and I had no real way of dealing with those experiences other than bottling my feelings inside. The police force did not have any programs or mechanisms to assist me in dealing with the trauma.

Furthermore, I saw the results of alcohol abuse and disconnected families. Often, people decided that suicide was the only solution to their struggles. I recall one incident where a young man, only eighteen years old, had just made the men's hockey team. He went home to share his exciting news with his family. When he arrived, however, they were intoxicated beyond belief. He took his own life with a firearm that was in their living quarters. When I heard the news, I was devastated. I was a member of the men's hockey team and I was proud of this young man's accomplishments. I knew that there was so much that he could have done if he had made a different choice. Well, I ended up having to transport his body to a larger urban centre—

an 8-hour drive in middle of winter—so that an autopsy could be performed. During that long, lonely drive, I kept asking myself what I could have done differently so that this tragic outcome didn't have to happen.

As you can imagine, I was deeply impacted by witnessing these tragedies. In fact, over the course of my career, I developed Post-Traumatic Stress or PTSD.4 The Mayo Clinic describes Post-Traumatic Stress as "a mental health condition that's triggered by a terrifying event—either experiencing it or witnessing it. Symptoms may include flashbacks, nightmares and severe anxiety, as well as uncontrollable thoughts about the event."5 In my case, I turned to alcohol as the way to deaden the pain that I was feeling from being surrounded by all this trauma and no way other than alcohol to deal with it. Alcohol plus alcohol induced bad behaviour resulted in me not being the sort of person that you would want to be around. My inner circle of friends became smaller as no one wished to be around me when my behaviour shifted. I found that self-isolation coupled with alcohol use was my go-to solution, when in fact it only made things worse. This kind of vicious circle is not uncommon. Mental illness and substance use—perhaps used as a coping mechanism, but an unhealthy one—often go hand in hand.

As the Mayo Clinic states, "many people who go through traumatic events may have temporary difficulty adjusting and coping, but with time and good self-care, they usually get better."6 However, this is not true for everyone. Some people find that their symptoms don't improve and may persist for "months or even years."7 A diagnosis of PTS usually includes symptoms that "interfere with your day-to-day functioning."8

Here is how the Mayo Clinic describes PTS symptoms:

PTSD symptoms are generally grouped into four types: intrusive memories, avoidance, negative changes in thinking and mood, and changes in physical and emotional reactions. Symptoms can vary over time or vary from person to person.9

Some examples of symptoms, according to the four types, are:

- Intrusive memories—flashbacks (reliving the event), upsetting dreams or nightmares, recurring and unwanted distressing memories of the traumatic event.
- Avoidance—trying to avoid thinking or talking about the event, avoiding places, people or activities that remind you of the event.
- Negative changes in thinking and mood—negative thoughts about yourself or other people, hopelessness about the future, memory problems, difficulty maintaining close relationships, difficulty experiencing positive emotions.
- Changes in physical and emotional reactions—easily startled or frightened, trouble sleeping, trouble concentrating, angry outbursts or aggressive behaviour.

Some symptoms can intensify over time, especially if they aren't dealt with when they first occur. For example, the simple backfire of a car's exhaust or fireworks can cause a person suffering from PTS to relive a combat experience. In my case, I suppose that if this story had stayed the course and I was a single person it may have a different ending. I was one of the lucky ones, though. Early in my career, I found the love of my life, Debra. We got married and had two wonderful children, Brandy and Mathew. You are probably wondering why I would share this information with you. It's because my family became the recipients of my bad behaviour as I struggled with dealing with what I now know as Post Traumatic Stress (PTS). I was not a good person to be around as my alcohol abuse continued to grow. Each place that we went to I experienced traumatic events some that would trigger other memories that I had locked away in my sub-conscious hoping to never visit again. There was no vent that I could expel all this pent-up negative energy except for the bottle of scotch that I thought was the elixir that would provide relief.

When the symptoms of PTS intensify, they can lead to suicidal thoughts. If you are working with someone as their mentor, it is important that you are aware of this shift and are prepared for what steps you must take to help this person get the professional help that they need. I highly recommend suicide intervention training for this reason. You want to make sure you have the tools that you need to address this. I took a couple of courses regarding suicide and I am forever grateful that I did. As a mentor I have added to my tool kit by so doing and can therefore provide additional support as people continue on their healing journey.

Some of the not so pleasant outcomes of PTS are: Intimate Partner Violence, caregiver burnout, compassion trauma and even developmental delay in youth who grow up in a home with one or more parent suffering from PTS.

Another type of mental health challenge that is directly related to careers in areas such as "law enforcement, combat, or any other service-related duties"[10] is Operational Stress Injury or OSI. eMentalHealth.ca describes an Operational Stress Injury as "any persistent psychological difficulty resulting from operational duties such as law enforcement, combat or any other service-related duties."[11]

I experienced PTS while engaged in law enforcement and even after that due to bullying in the workplace. It can surface in a number of ways. eMentalHealth outlines some of the causes of Operational Stress Injuries, which may include:

- Being involved in combat
- Witnessing atrocities
- Coming close to death
- Being assaulted
- Seeing someone killed or killing someone
- Being held hostage
- Natural disasters
- Handling injured bodies and human remains12

What I found interesting is that OSI is seen in those engaged in operational duties such as law enforcement, military, or other service-related duties. It can start as something as small as burnout or wear and tear and escalate from there.

It begs the question of whether a person has PTS or OSI. To better understand this, we need to look at OSI as something more specific to those engaged in service-related duties versus someone who was being bullied at work or in school and developed PTS as a result of that. PTS and mental health can come from a number of different places.

Some common types of OSI include:

- Post-Traumatic Stress Disorder (PTSD or PTS)
- Substance Use Disorders such as problems with alcohol and marijuana
- Anxiety Disorders, such as panic attacks and phobia
- Mood Disorders, such as problems with depression and anger13

There are many possible signs of an OSI, such as:

- Flashbacks—unwanted and vivid recollections of the event
- Poor sleep patterns coupled with nightmares
- Mood swings—anger, irritability
- Decrease in concentration
- Exaggerated startle response and hypervigilance
- Avoidance of people and places that remind one of the traumatic events
- Panic attacks and anxiety
- Loss of interest in activities14

WHERE DO WE FIND MENTAL HEALTH CHALLENGES?

We have likely all experienced some form of mental health challenges at some time point in our lives. For example, bullying is most often associated with children in school. But bullying can also occur within a family, especially if the relationships among the family members are unstable. If family members' love for each other is conditional—for example, if parents ask children to compete for their attention, creating sibling rivalries— then the family's role as part of each person's support structure is fractured. Instead of being part of the solution, the family becomes part of a person's struggles and challenges. This is so important and places a lot of responsibility on family members to be aware of the signs and signals. A failure to recognize problems can result in tragic outcomes.

Yet bullying is not limited to children or to families. It can happen anywhere that humans interact. This certainly includes the workplace! In fact, one area where many people's mental health suffers the most is in the workplace. Most organizations are not equipped to deal with or manage the challenges faced by their employees, and without direct care, those challenges only increase. A moderate amount of work which is well-paid and recognized by superiors and peers, and which contributes to the betterment of the world, can be good for a person's mental health. But if the workplace environment is negative, then the result can lead to physical and mental health problems.15

People with full-time jobs will spend upwards of 40 hours a week in their workplace, interacting with their coworkers and superiors. It's no surprise to find out that such a large proportion of people's everyday lives would have an important impact on their mental well-being. Yet many companies and organizations have no structures or processes in place to ensure that their employees feel safe and respected in speaking about and addressing any mental challenges they may face. As a result, depression and anxiety have a significant economic impact; the estimated cost to the global economy is US $1 trillion per year in lost productivity.16

THE WORLD HEALTH ORGANIZATION RECOGNIZES WORKPLACE STRESSORS AS IMPORTANT FACTORS IN MENTAL ILLNESS:

Bullying and psychological harassment (also known as "mobbing") are commonly reported causes of work-related stress by workers and present risks to the health of workers. They are associated with both psychological and physical problems. These health consequences can have costs for employers in terms of reduced productivity and increased staff turnover. They can also have a negative impact on family and social interactions.17

When I reflect back to the darkest time in my life, I now realize that I was also the subject of bullying by my superior, and a work environment that had caused me to internalize what I seen. That very same work environment did nothing to address the situation and did not provide me with tools to deal with the erosion of my mental health. I was not the only one that was exposed to workplace bullying, but I was one that had many other memories that I had bottled up sub-consciously and were sometimes triggered by the bullying.

If only companies and organizations recognized that "for every US $1 put into scaled up treatment for common mental disorders, there is a return of US $4 in improved health and productivity"[18]! If you were offered the opportunity for a four-fold return on investment, wouldn't you want to start investing your resources in that area? After all, harassment and bullying at work are commonly reported problems, and can have a substantial adverse impact on mental health. There are many effective actions that organizations can take to promote mental health in the workplace; such actions may also benefit productivity.

It is possible that as many as 2.5 million adult Canadians and 70,000 first responders have suffered from PTSD in their lifetimes. A recent study has estimated that productivity losses alone due to mental illness cost the Canadian economy $20.7 billion annually for a half-million workers.

www.Woundedwarriors.ca

MENTAL HEALTH AND MENTAL ILLNESS: WHAT'S THE DIFFERENCE?

Perhaps one reason many people don't recognize the impact of mental illness is because so few of us know about its opposite: mental health or mental well-being. As described by the Canadian Mental Health Association, "one in five people in Canada will experience a mental health problem or illness in any given year. But five in five of us have mental health."[19]

They go on to show the difference between the two states:

Mental illnesses are described as disturbances in thoughts, feelings, and perceptions that are severe enough to affect day-to-day functioning. Some examples are anxiety disorders, schizophrenia, and mood disorders, such as major depressive disorder and bipolar disorder. Mental health, however, is a state of well-being, and we all have it. Just like we each have a state of physical health, we also each have our mental health to look after. It's not just about surviving, it's about thriving. It's enjoying life, having a sense of purpose, and being able to manage life's highs and lows. Mental health isn't simply the absence of mental illness and living with a mental illness doesn't mean you can't have good mental health. Just like someone with diabetes, for example, can live a healthy life, so can somebody with a mental illness.[20]

My journey to mental health was not a quick or an easy one. However, I did ultimately make the changes in my life that were necessary. My wife Debra knew that there was a better person in my body. She and our children worked hard at getting me to see what that better person really looked like. They became that support structure that I needed, but it was certainly not pain free for them as they experienced all kinds of behaviour from me that they did not initiate. It ultimately required me to change my career. I left the police force as it was the cause of most of my trauma.

As I moved on with my career, there were triggers that would generate memories of events that had occurred which were unpleasant. Workplace bullying seemed to follow me on my career paths. Not knowing how to deal with these situations made things a lot worse. Not having the support from the workplace made things worse, almost as though the bad behaviour was being encouraged or at least tolerated. It follows the old story: if I am not told that my behaviour is incorrect, I therefore assume that it is acceptable. How wrong we were to embrace that thought process!

If you've experienced this kind of bullying or harassment, you're not alone. People are challenged at work, home, and in life dealing with strife in the workplace, depression, anxiety, most recently COVID-19, and many others.

But there is still hope! Picture a world where there is little or no issues with mental health or mental well-being. Picture organizations where the prevention of mental health and the negative effects of mental health are dealt with right at the onset, benefiting the individual and the organization. Imagine organizations and their leaders creating a safe place for you to work in and where prevention is the word rather than treatment. In this world, we have focused on the root cause of illness and have dealt with that without medication. In this world, your mentor is part of your support structure—standing beside you, not leaving you on the island by yourself. Your mentor is an active participant in your life, someone who will walk with you on your healing journey.

If you are one of the many people who are combating mental health problems, struggling towards mental well-being, or suffering from PTS or OSI, then this book offers one path you can follow. In reading this book, you will be guided by your mentor—me—so that you can begin and continue your healing journey. You will never have to go on this journey alone, because I will be at your side as your mentor.

If you are one of many mentors who want to make a difference, but you're sometimes not sure if you have the knowledge, skills, and abilities to make that difference, then this book is for you, too. You may not be comfortable yet in dealing with situations such as mental health or PTS. That is where this book will give you the tools that you need to feel more at ease in working with people who want to experience healing with you. Just imagine the feeling that you will get to experience by helping someone dealing with this turmoil. There is no greater reward than that.

CASE STUDY #1

As a young person attempting to change the world, Jean had been diagnosed with a couple of mental health issues. Her most recent one was that of being diagnosed as bi-polar. Jean had attempted suicide before and had moments where those thoughts would surface again. She had few friends and her support structure was minimal at best. She could talk with a couple of family members, but aside from that, her options were limited. Her attempts to get help through an online counseling service were more frustrating that helpful. She was placed on hold for long periods of time and then told to call back at another time. She felt as though she had been abandoned and had no real purpose. She was prone to rants with little or no meaning and this could be via text, email or in person. She was not receptive to being guided and actually would become more agitated if someone attempted to do so.

CASE STUDY #1 RESPONSE

Jean had been a part of a program that provided mentoring as one of the services that was offered to its participants. There seemed to be a connection between Jean and myself, even though she not been assigned to work with me. Despite a few attempts at reaching out to her she was not receptive to meeting and would cancel at a moment's notice. This seemed strange since there had been a connection between us at the outset. I recall doing a follow-up to see how Jean was doing, and it was at that point that she indicated that she wished to meet. Our first meeting was very much one-way, with her venting and me listening and attempting to provide guidance where I felt that I could. What was evident was that despite her struggle with mental health, she felt that she was in a better position to deal with her issues than I was. It was at this point that I reverted to a listen-only approach. I saw her demeanor change almost immediately. She wasn't as agitated. As a result of the change in my approach, she was sharing more of what she was going through.

She was an individual who had very low self-esteem and self-confidence. She was fearful of any type of relationship due to many failed relationships in her life. There was also some fear about any relationship that could become intimate due to how she had been treated growing up.

The approach that I took was as follows:
- Listen and hear what she was saying
- Refrain from offering guidance unless asked and then be selective when responding
- Manage when the meetings would take place—do not be at her beck and call
- Keep the meetings to a respectable time frame
- Watch for any indicators of becoming a crutch
- Watch for any indicators of her becoming suicidal
- Ascertain if she was seeking professional help and if so, what does that look like
- Remain non-judgmental

These steps can be applied with each mentoring relationship where you are working with someone who is dealing with mental health challenges. What I have found is that these steps can be applied in most if not all mentoring relationships.

3. IS THERE A SOLUTION?

The extensive problem that I described in the previous sections may seem insurmountable at first. The situation we're in now is desperate. More people need help more than ever. With so many people suffering, and with so many different causes and symptoms, how can we get to the root of the problem? We cannot leave people standing on an island by themselves. We need to demonstrate compassion and caring for those who are suffering. How can we help others to come to grips with their struggles and begin on a more positive, healthier path?

I believe that mentorship is the answer.

When I looked at the research, I found very few—if any—linkages between mentoring and mental health. That must change. I recently completed a workshop on suicide intervention (Applied Suicide Intervention Skills Training - LivingWorks (ASIST)) and found that my 11-plus years of mentoring experience were a valuable asset to me in the various situations that we explored. The feedback that I got from the participants validated for me that effective mentoring can and will make a difference in the mental health space. I have successfully completed the Applied Suicide Intervention Skills Training (ASIST) program to deepen my mentoring practice and strengthen the tools that I have in my mentoring tool kit. This goes along with other courses that I have taken to deepen my understanding of mental health, mental well-being and Post Traumatic Stress (PTS). I am also researching how mentoring can be part of the support structure for Operational Stress Injuries (OSI).

I have seen mentoring go through a paradigm shift. Today, the best kind of mentorship is a two-way, trusted relationship where both the mentor and mentee are able to learn and grow on both a personal and professional basis. Mentorship has become a relationship that spans geographies, sectors, genders and generations. Mentoring is not about a particular outcome or destination; it's a professional journey. It's a process of discovery, not just ladder-climbing.

As more and more people and organizations turn to mentoring as a viable solution to challenges that they are dealing with we need to ramp up our knowledge, skills and abilities as an effective mentor. Mentoring is the difference and mentoring can be a part of the support structure. For so long we have sought help from hospitals, social workers, psychiatrists, therapists, and counselors. But now, we can recognize mentoring as the differentiation.

We need to be effective mentors and become part of the support structure that is combating mental health, mental well-being, PTS, and OSI. This has gone on for far too long and now is the time to step up and be part of the healing process. This book will provide you with the tools that you need to begin that journey.

THE MENTORING COMMUNITY

The mentoring community has grown extraordinarily in just a few short years!

When I think of what we are doing I reflect back to the earlier days of my journey. I recall a prominent consulting organization that offered to purchase the Intellectual Property Rights to what I had in place for mentor certification as well as the services that I was offering. They would hire me as the Director of Mentoring Services and have me deliver what I had built under their branding. Something told me to not go there and to stay the course for bigger and better things. Mentoring, when afforded the opportunity, can create the opportunity for great things to happen. This was just one of those situations.

On reflection, what I have found is that the majority of the solutions that I provide are a blend of mentoring and leadership. The skills to be a great leader are similar to that of a great mentor. With the development of my mentoring practice, I am also recognized as a thought leader in the mentoring space. I devote part of my working day to responding to questions relating to the practice of mentoring which includes process, concepts and the application of each of these in various situations.

I remember a number of years ago when I did my market research on mentoring and mentor certification. I found that there were lots of solution providers who claimed that if you took their training that you would be certified. What I saw was a solution provider that provided a blend of technology and process solutions (mentoring programs). A lot were cookie cutter solutions and were not customized to the organization. I found that the certification offered was in fact self-certification. There was not an independent body to certify mentors. My vision was that we would have an independent body for the certification of mentors. That we would have standards in place for the delivery of mentoring. We would certify mentors based on competence and not on an exam to test their knowledge. The certification more appropriately would be a blend of the two. Hence the formation of the International Mentoring Community in 2017 – an independent body for the certification of mentors.

To be certified as competent as a mentor requires that you not only have the knowledge but that you can apply that knowledge in a practical sense. The more hours you have, the more reflection you have, the deeper your knowledge of mentoring practices will be.

I have developed a Practice of Mentoring and I deliver a number of services as part of that practice. All of these services are intended to bring value to people and to organizations. Part of the responsibility of having a Mentoring Practice requires that I constantly evolve the practice of mentoring and the process and the concepts of mentoring. I am continually looking for ways to enhance my skills and abilities through various professional development opportunities. As a professional mentor practitioner, I need to gain an understanding of the pain points that my clients are dealing with. I have to explore solutions that I can provide that are mentoring-related.

As part of developing my practice, I am an internationally certified mentor. I have completed my Certificate of Achievement – Mentoring and my Certificate of Competence – Mentor from the International Mentoring Community (IMC). Most recently, I have completed my Certificate of Competence – Journey Mentor which focuses on mentoring individuals through the Mentor Certification process and has a primary focus on mentoring as a part of the support structure for mental health, mental well-being and Post Traumatic Stress (PTS) and Operational Stress Injury (OSI).

I have led teams and mentored individuals for over 2,500 logged mentoring hours, with 32 industries and over 1200 individuals. Furthermore, I worked over 25,000 hours in the field of mentoring itself, as a speaker, author, facilitator, trainer, researcher, and practitioner. I consistently place in Quora's Top 10 'Most Viewed Writers' for 'Mentors and Mentoring' and 'Business Mentoring,' where I provide my knowledge and expertise to the masses.

I launched my mentoring company, TalentC, in 2009, and I published The Gift of Mentoring in 2014. In 2018, I co-founded the International Mentoring Community (IMC).

YET BEYOND THESE QUALIFICATIONS, WHAT DO I HAVE TO OFFER THAT WOULD SET ME APART FROM OTHERS?

I have experienced PTS and have battled through it to recognize that more needed to be done. I was one of a small group who were fortunate to have a strong support group – but not everyone does. This book is part of my journey. I am taking the first steps towards helping others in their healing process. I will help you understand how mentoring can be part of your support structure. You just need to reach out and ask for help.

I believe that I can show you how mentoring can become an integral part of anyone's mental health and mental well-being.

This book is for the individual that is suffering/struggling with mental health, poor mental well-being, PTS, and OSI. You do not need to suffer without a support group. You need to reach out to your mentor to get the support that you need. Your mentor will have access to a resource pool of professionals that can work with you to address the suffering and anguish that you are experiencing today. You do not need to go on this journey on your own. Now is the time if any to reach out to your mentor and say the words, "Help me!"

Finally, this book is for all the mentors out there that want to make a difference in the world and want to be able to be part of the support structure that we have talked about. Now is the time for you to take that step and to guide that person suffering from mental health challenges, poor mental well-being, PTS, and OSI to a place of healing with you by their side.

Do not despair! There are solutions out there that can help with the healing process that do not need to be cloaked in a stigma.

One of those solutions is mentoring. I know that you have a ton of questions as to what is mentoring and how would it be of any value in being part of the support structure for these illnesses. I have been mentoring most of my life; training others to mentor, speaking about the power of mentoring, mentoring at all levels and mentoring in over 30+ industries.

I want to take you on a journey with this book. I will answer the questions that you have concerning "what is mentoring?" and I will show you how mentoring can be part of that support struggle. Mentoring can and will be a solution to a failing support structure.

RECOGNIZING THE PROBLEM: DAWN'S STORY

In this section, I'll give the floor to a colleague whose personal experience with mentoring has shaped her experiences and who she is as a person. Her lived experiences help paint the picture of what we are really dealing with—and how mentorship can help. Dawn writes:

I was physically ill, emotionally broken and spiritually disconnected when I showed up on her doorstep. I didn't know it yet, but the woman I was about to meet would have a profound impact on my life. Not only would she teach me how to listen to my body and give me tools to restore my failing health, but she'd also address my complete lack of self-esteem, unhappiness and perpetual fear of living. The mentoring I received from her more than twenty years ago is the reason why I'm alive and well today.

I will never forget the first time I sat in her office. She was very different from anyone else I had met. For the first time since I had been facing these unusual immune system challenges, I felt listened to and understood. This 60-year-old woman, with a no-nonsense haircut and practical dress, wasn't a medical professional, and yet she managed to ease my symptoms in one hour. This was something the medical professionals had not been able to accomplish thus far, but Theresa, had been taught the art of natural healing by some very prominent mentors.

One of Theresa's mentors was a biochemist, physician. and psychiatrist, who not only helped her heal from schizophrenia, but won the Nobel Prize for his research with the disease. Another was a scientist and Nobel Prize winner twice over, and the third was an old Irish priest who was known for his teachings on self-awareness. There was no question that Theresa's success—her books, reputation and acclaim in the Orthomolecular Hall of Fame—was due in part to her lineage of brilliant mentors.

Mentoring is a gift that touches many lives. It is like a stone cast into a still pond, in which the water ripples out far and wide. Theresa touched many lives with her mentoring and I happened to be one of those fortunate individuals who has had the privilege of carrying on that torch.

I will never forget the day I sat in her office feeling so frustrated that I was fighting back the tears. "I'm certain that I'm one of your best clients," I said. "I follow your program to the last detail." I might add that Theresa's regime wasn't an easy one, but I was desperate and terrified of what my fate might be if I didn't comply. At age 27, I'd lost all vitality, had a host of health issues and was struggling to keep weight on my scrawny frame, but what concerned me the most was what would happen to my 3-year-old if I didn't sort this out.

Theresa looked at me for a long moment and then she said, "You need to do some emotional work." Taken aback and slightly offended, I thought to myself, "There's nothing wrong with me emotionally!" Little did I know that I had loads of personal growth and healing to do. So much, in fact, that my body couldn't get well because all of my vitality was being hijacked by my deep hurts, fear, low self-esteem and unhappy existence. Sadly, I didn't realize there was anything that needed fixing because I hadn't known anything better. As far as I was concerned, life was just a joyless struggle, but Theresa was about to put a new idea on my radar.

Theresa peered over her glasses, waiting for my response. Nothing escaped her attention and she noted my recoil at her suggestion. She immediately backed off saying, "Take some time to think about it."

My mind was reeling. "What other options do I have?" So far, she was the only person who was able to get any favorable results with me. "What do you want me to do?" I asked her.

"Fill this notebook with your life story and get back to me when you're done," she said.

That was the opening of a brand-new world for me. This wise woman taught me a level of self-awareness that I couldn't have achieved on my own. She asked me profound questions, honored my deep hurts and showed me where my beliefs caused more pain than good. She never told me what to do, but rather, she gently encouraged me to access my own inner wisdom. By the time our mentoring relationship came to an end about 5 years later, I was healthier than I had ever been, and had a sense of love and acceptance for myself, something I had not previously known. I ventured out into my expanded world equipped with a new understanding of myself and a toolkit to slay any dragons I might encounter along the way.

Perhaps one of the most exquisite pieces of wisdom I took from my time working with Theresa was that, as long as we approach a problem in the same way, we will continue to reap the same results. Nothing boggled my mind more than watching her work miracles, proving beyond any doubt that her suggestions got results, and then watching those same recipients go home feeling great, only to slide right back into their old ways. I always found it curious, watching people stubbornly digging in their heels, trying to get the universal laws to bend to their will rather than aligning with how they actually work. It took me years of working with my own clients to fully understand what underlies this resistance. In short, the mind is our biggest obstacle when it comes to personal growth and healing.

Years ago, I taught classes about the fear of failure using EFT Tapping. EFT is a natural healing modality based on the principles of acupuncture and has the effect of releasing stress and trauma from the body. At the start of each class, we'd work on releasing the participant's fear of failing. As the fear of failing subsided, they'd inevitably tell me that a new fear had arisen in its place, and it was the fear of success.

Once again, we'd work through the fear of success—the fear of the unknown and the discomfort success would bring.

Finally, when those fears subsided, one last existential fear would surface. They'd ask, "Who am I?"

For most of their lives, they had told themselves that there was no point in trying because they'd certainly fail. Essentially, they identified themselves as failures, but when that belief suddenly collapsed and they were on the cusp of change, envisioning success as a real possibility, they were met with resistance once again. They'd express hesitation in letting go of their old identity telling me, "But this is who I've been for my entire life! This is my story! Who will I be when I let this go?"

Your history, with all its wonderful wisdom, will always be a part of you. What doesn't need to be a part of you is the pain and limiting beliefs you drag around year after year because you keep telling yourself that old story is still who you are. It certainly doesn't have to be. Why not live something big, bold and new? Why continue to entrench yourself in pain and limiting beliefs just because they are familiar, when you can have something better instead?

Perhaps it seems counterproductive, but when I mentor people, I'm always looking at the pain points in their lives. I'm not concerned with the things that are working well for them, but rather, I'm interested in the pain, struggles and stress. I want to know why my client's aspirations are just dreams instead of realities. The job of a mentor is to help you identify and release your inner obstacles, because without the pains, fears, insecurities and limiting beliefs, there's nothing but an open road to achieving your goals.

We've all come here with gifts to share that flow effortlessly from our true selves. The tricky part, is to undo the old programming that tells us we aren't smart enough, good enough or deserving enough to have what we long for.

Years ago, I had a client who had left a good job as an administrator because, she said, "It was sucking my soul." As we talked, she described how she had been out of work for years and she had almost burned through her savings. She had started applying for admin jobs and found it odd that she hadn't had one call for an interview.

The next thing I asked, impacted her deeply. "This is what I'm hearing, please correct me if I'm wrong," I said. "You want to get a job because you need an income, but you hate working as an administrator. You're applying for admin jobs, but everything in you is screaming, 'No!' Essentially, you have one foot on the gas pedal and the other on the brake, and you're wondering why your car isn't moving."

The woman was almost in tears at the realization. Indeed, she had been sabotaging her success because she couldn't imagine doing anything else other than the job she despised. People tend to get stuck in patterns of thoughts and mentoring can be a valuable tool to help people break out of that old mental programming.

TAKING THE FIRST STEP: DESIREE'S STORY

The first step of a journey is always the point at which we recognize that the journey is necessary. In the case of mentorship, this can mean the decision to stop our progress down a previous path and turning onto a more difficult—but more rewarding—way.

Here is another personal account from Desiree, who recounts how mentoring helped her during the onset of COVID-19. As Desiree realized that her entire world was changing, she also recognized some signs within herself that pointed her in a new direction. With a dedicated mentor, Desiree was able to work back towards a state of mental well-being. Desiree writes:

From early days, basically, I had heard about COVID happening and had personal experience of it happening to friends living internationally quite a few months before it started affecting myself personally and people in my environment. I had friends that were living in China and got stuck outside of China when COVID was just starting to hit and they actually came to visit me in another country, so my friends were in China, they went to Canada, COVID started, they came down to Panama to visit me while they were waiting to try to get back in the country.

It's an interesting reflection point to look back at that time. That was in January when that was happening. We had thorough conversations with the information that we had, knowing what was going on intensely in China. We still made very, what I would say now is naive assumptions that it would stay localized and that that situation was going to get handled, it wasn't a big deal, and we were all just going to return to our lives. Everything's fine.

I spent time with them for maybe a week. They eventually made their way back to China, so we're talking maybe end of January at this point in time. For myself, my year plans were to do quite a bit of travel. When they departed, I departed to Costa Rica to go do a festival and connect with humans. I'm somebody that is very human-centric and I was really, really looking forward to that event and had planned it a year in advance. This was the first festival that I was going to. Amazing. Finally made time in my schedule to go do that.

Still, at the time, looking back, the pandemic had already been spreading. We knew about this. It was in Europe, it was starting to get into the US, and still not a concern, personally, which is interesting in terms of what your worldview is to your threat to yourself versus society. Even being a very externally-focused person and worried about world issues, there still wasn't that full concept.

From there, I went to Costa Rica, went to this festival with thousands and thousands of people. This was the last festival in the world that completed as COVID started to come through, but you would never have known. We're outdoors, people are there. It's yoga, it's music, everyone's hugging. Everybody is connected in this very profound human way. Looking back, I'm very grateful for that experience because that filled up my tank of human nature interaction, not knowing what I was going into shortly after.

Then it happened. That was mid to end of February. I stayed in Costa Rica after the festival for a couple of weeks, but then you were starting to see the news and you're starting to realize things are coming in a little bit closer, things are coming in a little bit closer, but we don't have a lot of information really, truly about what COVID is at this time, so you're like, "Eh, it's okay. It's out there." Keeping an eye on it, keeping an eye on government responses, and knowing that borders are starting to close, I should pay attention to this, but again, still not feeling personally concerned.

I ended up coming back to Panama three days before the borders closed, which in hindsight, that was cutting it close, but it seemed fine. I was around people from Europe and all over the place and they were coming in from France and from Germany and from all of these hotspots probably exposed to COVID, and then come back, had one normal day, and then everything changed. From there, that's when things ramped up in intensity. I don't know if we want to just dive into what that looked like from a social perspective, but there's quite a few stories that happen as that started to ramp up personally.

I have a very international friend group, and that means that you've got personalities from around the world. You've got cultural perspectives from around the world and we're a very social friend group, get together a lot, and so we always have plans on the go, and so come back to Panama, go for a hike with friends, go for breakfast, go for coffee, all of this is happening. The girls were planning a trip to just go out to an island for an afternoon and come back. Cool, except COVID's starting to happen and people are starting to get nervous and you can start to feel the energy is changing in society, and so I'm going and getting my basic supplies, knowing something could change awful fast here. I'm starting to ramp up my supplies, starting to be more cautious.

I go out for dinner with one friend, they're starting to do sanitation at the restaurant. We come out of the restaurant at night and there's the parking lot for the grocery store next door is full. There were people parked on the streets. You can feel the intensity. I'm still not personally processing this at this point in time of what's coming next, and with a friend from Panama, and so she has more of a worldview of how extreme the government can get, and so we're finishing up dinner, we're standing on the street talking, she gives me a hug, and she's like... Oh, I paid for dinner, and she was like, "Don't do that. I don't know what I'm going to see you again." I'm like, "What do you mean you don't know when you're going to see me again?" She was just like, "I don't know. I don't feel good about this." Give her a hug and she's like, "Goodbye, friend, because I don't know when I'm going to see you again."

It hit me weird and in hindsight, she had a lot better insight into what was probably going to come than I did because of different cultural perspectives. At the same time, the rest of my international friend group is like, "Hey, let's go. Let's go out. Let's go to this island. Let's have a good time." These girls are planning this trip and I'm like, "Mm, I've got enough indicators that this is a bad idea." We have a friend that's just returned from Brazil, she's like, "Hey, girls. I feel like I've been exposed. I can't come on this trip because I don't want to put you at risk." I said, "Good call." In the chat group, I said, "Thank you. Keep us safe." Other friends of mine attacked me at that point. They were like, "Well, you're not being inclusive," and things got very tense. You could start to feel the anger ramping up.

That's where you started to see those different shifts in cultural perspective. People from different cultures were reacting differently. Some people were being hypervigilant. Some people were being overly paranoid about the government. Some people were angry that their lives were changed and like, "We can't be restricted." This started to get tense among my friends who are very open-minded, highly educated, free-loving, very, very human-centered people, and you can see personalities change overnight, and I stepped back.

It felt weird to step back because you're wanting to socially connect because you know that you're going through a stressful situation, and so my personal inclination, single, I live alone, is to connect with my friends and my social group. But now you're at that odd of, I don't think it's safe to connect physically, but it's also not feeling safe to connect emotionally, and so you're kind of like, "Okay, this is the first time that I need to step back and protect myself." Then that gets to be psychologically weird because you are in a situation where myself, I typically am somebody that is a mentor, a supporter of my friend group, that person that people call for support, and I'm starting to shift into that space where I need support.

It's a weird mental space to be in. Logically, I can look at it and understand that it's okay. It's okay to need that social support, but it's a weird shift to be the needer of the receiving, and so I'm starting to pull back. I'm also feeling guilty because I'm not showing up for my friends and I'm not showing up for other people. Then other people around the world, friends are starting to break down and have stresses and reach out and I'm having to set boundaries, say "No, I can't help you right now. What other supports do you have?" There was some resistance from that, but people understood, so there wasn't pressure, but it was just weird. They still just kept reaching out because they're used to me providing that support, so then you keep feeling guilty.

There was a period of time where, I believe it was maybe two weeks, as things started to get really intense and of March early April. My phone rang with messages 24 hours a day for about two weeks because I have friends in every time zone, so every time somebody was awake, somebody was having a trauma and I was having a trauma. I also couldn't reach out to those friends because they couldn't show up for me, I couldn't show up for them. Everyone is just throwing this energy and it's all hectic, stressful, anxious energy happening.

I remember just researching online how do I put an out-of-office reply on my text messages so that I'm still telling people that I show up for them, but I can't right now. I just couldn't do it and I got to the point that I had to ignore people and that felt, again, bad, guilty, and so that was really intense. That shifted again, I would say, maybe two to four weeks later where friends would start to reach out. They're looking for some stability point. They're used to me having a plan, so okay, I'm usually the person with the plan, but my plans have all fallen apart for the year, so I've had to cancel my entire year, travel, financial plans, possibly job plans coming up, family plans, the whole thing.

I have enough perspective and I've done enough coaching that I understand that that's okay not to have plans right now. I can give myself that kind of space. I didn't give myself the space to lower my expectations of myself during this period of high intensity, so I still had these high expectations to come up with the right answer, but I knew it was okay not to have the whole plan. Friends would start reaching out. They're looking for stability and they'd say, "Hey, what's your plans for change? Are you moving countries? Are you changing jobs? What are you going to do next year? What would you like your life to look like now that there's this opportunity for change?" But they weren't asking because they were curious what my worldview was or what my plans were for change, they were asking because they wanted to hear somebody say something reassuring, somebody that they trust having a plan would make them feel good right now, because then things feel more in control.

But then I couldn't give them that, and so when I would respond and say, "I don't know," and I have to stand in this space of not knowing, and I don't know the end date of when I'm going to know again, and this is how it is, that would be met with resistance, but you always, "No, but what do you think? Can you hypothesize a bit?" "No." Then that's when it would come up that they were feeling out of control on their side.

In this stage, I had very good people in my life reaching out because I started to pull back from social interactions. I don't think I have ever in my life been in a situation where I personally have pulled back from social interactions, but because the intensity was ramping up and because every interaction with somebody wanting reassurance or wanting to express their stress, I didn't have the capacity, and so I started to retreat, which, again, at face value, I understand that that's not necessarily healthy, but there was a level of protection mechanism happening.

I had very good friends that are socially aware, high emotional intelligence, some friends, some past intimate partners. Everyone's in different places in the world, everyone's stuck in their own circumstance, but there were a few core people that really went out of their way, even during their own trauma, to recognize and realize I was alone, solo, isolated, probably not doing well and not checking in and truly did set a cadence of reaching out to check in: "Are you okay? I understand that. Like I've been going through this, you're probably feeling this similar emotion. What are you doing about that within a family context that I know you have or within a friend context that I know you have? Have you taken care of yourself with X, Y, Z thing?"

Those conversations were invaluable because I wasn't going to reach out for that support in the way that I needed to and that was the time that those key people actually did step up and provide that mutual support that I had provided to them in the past, so that really helped to define those social structures, but it really changed the interaction because all of this was being done online and you're completely removed from any intimacy, any touch, any social interaction in the way that we knew it before. Add screen time, working online eight to 10 hours a day, and then the only way that you can connect with people again is screen time, and so that layer made it feel both exhausting and like work to have that connection.

We had a psychologist speak at work in regards to Zoom and the delays of facial expressions, so you're not getting quite that same feedback. Your brain is really processing on a slower basis, and so it was exhausting but necessary at the same time. In my circumstance, we couldn't see people at all, so at one point of the pandemic, I would say between mid to end of March till June, three or four months, I hadn't seen a single person that I knew. Although possible, not ideal for somebody who processes anxiety through physical touch, through social connection and through those types of distractions, so all of that was affecting sleep. That's where you start to get into somatic things, PTSD, all of those types of responses, and so I would say closer to the end of that full social isolation, three or four-month-mark, I could start to feel it in my body.

I'm always a very academic person when it comes to analyzing psychological impact, coaching, social awareness, all of these types of things for myself, I could feel it shift from being able to just observe as an observer and analyze to feeling the trauma in my body at that point, because there was no way to get the anxiety or the stress taken care of, and so it started to affect sleep. For the first four months of the pandemic, I couldn't get more than four hours of sleep at night. I was lucky if I got five. That pattern has stayed with me, unfortunately, so I moved that from four hours to five hours. Okay, great. When I started to be able to push that sleep to even, say, six hours, I still woke up at, well, between 2:00 and 4:00 in the morning every night for probably eight months.

I have now removed myself from a lot of these traumatic physical scenarios, if we fast forward to the future, but I still have that stress response, and so if I am stressed, it's not a hundred percent of the time, but I am still having to reprogram my sleeping and be very, very conscious of it: good sleep hygiene, stress management, those types of things. I think that that is going to stay for quite some time.

Intimacy side as well, there just got to be to the point that there's no intimacy available. You can't legally meet people. You can't physically do that, so although I could shift some of those intimacy pieces to online connection, it's not the same, you're not receiving touch, and so that just was an outstanding issue through the year, remains an issue.

I mean, those types of things are shifting the way that we're interacting and as somebody that's single and dating, those types of things, I think on a society level, we're going to see a shift of types of communication needed, possibly for the better. We do need to verbally communicate our needs now more, we need to communicate our safety. We need to do things that we should have been doing all along and clarifying for respect with people, but we have a physical health piece that we can see in front of all of us now that's a common point. Those who are not strong with communicating are still taking risks and those who are strong with communicating or having that tough conversation and making decisions and having to be vulnerable before meeting, but it does change the types of interactions and how that relationship may develop.

The intimacy piece was tough and I think that that just left me in a state of anxiety that I couldn't resolve for months and months and months and months and months. I don't know when that's fully going to resolve. I think that even if friendships come back and partnerships come back and more physical time around people come back, I think that it's going to be a long time for that to build to a level of consistency again.

It's the theory of, is your cup half-full or full or empty? People's cups have been depleted so much that I think we're in an instant gratification culture where we're used to fixing things, getting information really fast, and these types of self-development pieces and connection pieces that we're going to have to recover from are going to take much longer than society deems acceptable for attaching to a certain topic. We don't think about things for this long, so I think people are going to need different strategies and I'm working on it myself to just understand that there are stages of progression of dealing with this and you're going to have these regression points, you're going to have these growth points, and just try to find that middle balance as you cope, so lots around that. I don't know if there's anything there that you really want to dig into. I can probably go into some coping mechanisms, stuff like that as well.

I'll be the first to admit that my coping mechanisms were less than ideal. I think that this is one of the most stressful times that I've probably ever experienced. I'm not shy of stress, but it got to the point where I'm not a substance user at all, I live a very clean lifestyle, it got to the point where I was like, "Yeah, I'm going to either choose to pick my poison tonight. Is that going to be a glass of wine? Is that going to be anti-anxiety medication? Is that going to be CBD?" Whatever that case is and staying conscious of it, not using anything in excess, but there got to be points of anxiety that you could feel your brain's not functioning anymore. Now is the time that you actually do need to lean on medical support.

I can understand people's resistance with those types of things, because you don't want to create a dependency. Those types of supports are there for a reason and it's really important for people to recognize when you should do that. When do you need antidepressant medication? When do you need anti-anxiety medication? Those types of things that you can own for yourself and take responsibility for yourself, because nobody can force you to do that, but it's also a fine balance of doing it when you need it, making sure that you're doing that responsibly, so I had to stay quite conscious of that throughout.

I had issues with eating for the first few months. I couldn't eat. I lost possibly... Yeah, I checked at my doctor. I lost 20 pounds through the first part of the pandemic, which it wasn't from exercise, it was from anxiety, so there were all those physical factors happening. Tying that into where does mentorship fit in this? There are these things that you can own. You have to be responsible for your own well-being for making those choices for seeking medical help when you need, for not falling into bad habits, for recognizing habits. You can have all the knowledge in the world, but without those people guiding you, holding you accountable, you're going to have a lot tougher time, and so earlier in the conversation I mentioned, I've got this core group of people that were checking in. I don't necessarily have formal mentorship relationships with those people, but I do have mutually shared mentorship relationships with those people.

I'm very, very lucky to have this group of individuals that I've chosen to be in my life and chosen as a core of my life that are emotionally intelligent, understand the core principles of either coaching, mentorship. They do these types of things in their work, et cetera, that was central to me becoming attached to healthy behaviors and keeping me accountable. I probably wasn't going to fall off the rails. I wasn't truly at risk of that, but it helps to have those attachment points.

I had to seek as well mentorship and connection outside of my typical circle because everybody was going through stress, and so I found myself in a situation where I haven't attached to formal psychology counseling before those types of things. I often do this informally because of the benefit of my network, but my network wasn't functioning at full capacity, so what I ended up doing was connecting with a group based in New York that would get together once a week online, Zoom, people from around the world would join and they would share stories of human connection, and that group, because it was a group of strangers, it was a safe space for people to share positive things, sad things, whatever was happening, and just have this conversation circle. You could participate, you didn't need to. It ended with some music and some everyone dancing in their house and whatever and it was really cute and it was really nice. It was that glimmer of hope to see that people were showing up for each other, even if they didn't know each other.

I would count that as a type of mentorship or a group mentorship that happened informally that provided safe space for people that were isolated or not, but they just needed to talk, and that became a consistent. It's something that I didn't tell other people that I was doing. I didn't want other people to come to my group. It was just this nice, quiet safe space where you didn't have to put on the front and be strong for other people, you could do better, so that group mentorship became very central and it provided a really good consistency point.

I, in the future, probably need to look at formal counseling just because there are going to be long-term effects as well and I'm finally getting to the point, and this is an interesting point, too, is how much energy do you have to seek mentorship and to seek support while you're going through trauma. We know that you should, as a practitioner of it, as somebody who provides mentorship to people, I know that you should put the energy. When you're depleted on energy and you're like, "I can't do this," that's when you need it the most. But I myself failed at that miserably because we're human and I couldn't bring myself to have those formal conversations while that trauma was happening, and so the safe way was to attach to that casual mentorship and to do those check-ins with people.

Fast forward, I'm in a different stage. I am coming back to some level of energy. I'm in a safer environment. The immediate burden of everything is starting to dissipate, and so now it's time to attach to more formal structure with that and to make sure that that keeps going because otherwise, you kind of just sit in this in-between space, and if you're in this in-between space, you're fine, but you're not actively healing from what happened and you're not growing. Mentorship is nice because it's looking at the whole person. You're not necessarily just looking to coach to solve one problem, you're not necessarily looking at psychology to work on a certain behavior, say cognitive behavior therapy or something like that.

That mentorship piece is nice because it provides that in-between, it knows when the psychology is aligned and you need that professional support for that behavior, for that sleep pattern, or whatever that case is. It knows the line of, "Hey, is this affecting your performance in something that you're wanting to achieve?" You can dive into that if you want, but it really is looking at the whole person, which I think is what we need right now, collectively as society. Yes, individually, we need this a little bit, but collectively as society, that mentorship piece should be, I would argue, core in all of our interactions, whether you name it that or not.

Are we looking at the person as a whole person? Are we asking them questions? Are we just giving them space to process themselves? Because people at their core also know what their challenges are right now, but just might not have a space or somebody to articulate that to and that might be all they need is just somebody to say, "Hey, what's going on for you?" Then that gives them the space to make a choice of what to do with that once they can articulate what's going on with them, so I think that, yeah, mentorship is key to moving things forward, professionally, personally, whatever this is collectively as a group, but it is that way to provide a container, I guess, around however we move forward with this.

4. WHAT IS A MENTOR?

As Dawn's and Desiree's stories have shown, a positive mentorship can be life-changing. But what is the history of mentorship, and how has it changed in today's world?

THE HISTORY OF MENTORSHIP

Mentoring has evolved over the many years that it has been in existence. The term "mentor" originated with the character of Mentor in Homer's Odyssey, which dates back around 3000 years. In this epic story, the hero Odysseus entrusts his young son Telemachus to the care of Mentor, his trusted companion. Mentor is able to encourage and support Telemachus in discovering what has happened to his father, and help him return to his kingship after many years away. This history of a person who is able to support and encourage a young person to grow and mature is where we get the term "mentor" today.

Mentorship also has a historical link to Middle Ages, when young people were accepted as apprentices into guilds of knowledgeable journeymen and masters. The apprentices worked for the masters as they gradually developed their skills and learned the tricks of the trade. This image is probably the most common one that we have today when we think of "mentorship". We probably envision a more senior person (like a grey-haired guru perched atop a mountain) passing on their wisdom and knowledge by "telling" their younger mentee how to solve a problem.

People are now looking at mentoring in a different light. Mentoring in the twenty-first century has become "effective mentoring." The terminology "effective mentoring" is clearly indicative of the paradigm shift that I mentioned earlier. There are a number of components (process and concepts) that are now part of being an effective mentor. When I look at where mentoring has come from and where it is today the change has been phenomenal—it has become what it is today because of it being recognized as a viable business solution.

Let's clear up a myth about mentoring so that we all start on the same page. This term that I am about to mention is one that is a pet peeve of mine. Every so often you hear the term "reverse mentoring." This typically refers to situations where a younger person is mentoring a much older person. We see this when it comes to technology. The younger person guides a much older person through the technological world. As you are reading this part of the book, I want you to wipe the term "reverse mentoring" from your memory bank. You are probably wondering why. The word "reverse" means to go backwards. Now I am not sure about you, but I don't want any of the mentoring that I do to be seen as going backwards! Besides all of that, effective mentoring—a two-way trusted relationship seems to have a better meaning than the "reverse mentoring" label. This style of mentoring still exists today but it is now referred to as "effective mentoring."

Mentors and mentees build relationships where it is a win-win situation. In other words, the mentor and mentee both come away from this experience having learned something about themselves and about their career path. An effective mentor will spend time focusing on the personal growth of their mentee (and their own growth) before they address anything to do with the career path.

A mentor is someone who will guide—not tell—and who is very adept at asking questions rather than telling. This is referred to as the Socratic Method. An effective mentor will ask a series of questions that will guide the mentee to the answer. They help with the development of critical thinking skills. An effective mentor is an effective communicator as well.

WHY IS COMPETENCE SO IMPORTANT?

Mentoring in its purest form can help individuals navigate through life changing/life altering situations. We fear the unknown and we fear change but your mentor will walk beside you as you go on your personal journey. Your mentor, if competent, will guide you to the answers of all the questions that you may have but they will not tell you. A competent mentor can provide a deeper, richer mentoring experience. They have the lived experiences that they are willing to share that will bring clarity to your road map.

To be certified as a competent mentor, you will be verified against a number of Action_Outcome statements (competency statements) and are required to demonstrate that you have applied your knowledge for each Action_Outcome statement. An example of an Action_Outcome statement would be, "Discuss the importance of cognitive-affective issue indicators." This doesn't have to be a daunting task if you have been keeping a mentoring log. I update my mentor log as soon as possible after a mentoring engagement/session. I also use that log to refresh my memory on what we had talked about in the last session.

The competence of a mentor is important but it is even more important when it comes to mentoring in the mental health space. You are not prescribing. You are not diagnosing. You are listening and hearing and offering support. You can be an integral part of the support structure. I have had so many people tell me how it would have been beneficial to their healing if they had a mentor who was competent and comfortable working in the mental health space. We need to listen and hear what people are saying and develop competent mentors who are comfortable in the mental health space.

THE SCALE OF EFFECTIVE MENTORSHIP

When I was researching material for this book and increasing my Practice of Mentoring to include mental health, mental well-being and PTS, I created this hierarchy for mentoring. This approach is similar to what we see in some of the leadership literature but it has never been expanded to the mentoring space. Take a few moments to read through the descriptors for mentor, great mentor, and extraordinary mentor.

MENTOR

We have all had a mentor in our life at some time point. It could have been a family member, a teacher, someone in the workplace, or someone who was assigned to mentor us as part of a corporate mentorship program. Our mentor was a highly capable person that provided us with the answers to all our questions. There was a sense that they wanted to do more but did not have all the tools to be able to do so. When crunched for time, a mentor will sometimes lose sight of the journey and their role in guiding the person they are spending time with.

As a mentor, we sometimes take the easy road and may not utilize proper mentoring processes. The one that I see most often is "telling" your mentee what they need to do rather than asking a series of questions that will guide them to the answer. A mentor may struggle with the concept that mentoring is a two-way trusted relationship where the mentor and mentee will learn and grow together on a personal and professional basis. I just finished a virtual networking event where the majority of the mentors were focused on creating agendas, assigning tasks and not taking the time to find out more about the person that they are mentoring. In all my years of mentoring and the countless hours I have done, I have always started the relationship with addressing my mentee's personal growth. How can you market and sell something if you do not believe in yourself and the product or service that you are delivering to your clients? Sometimes we lose sight of what this is all about. It is not about you. Your focus needs to be on the person that you are spending time with as their mentor.

When I look at the hierarchy of mentoring, the "mentor" is the first step one can take to helping someone become the best that they can be. It is your beginning of a mentoring relationship that will have a life changing impact on those that you touch.

GREAT MENTOR

A great mentor is someone that you immediately think about when asked who your mentor is. They navigate effectively and efficiently through the mentoring process to guide and encourage the person they are spending time with to success. They have a good understanding of the concepts and are able to apply those concepts in a mentoring arrangement. They have had some formal training and take pride in their ability to continue to learn. They embrace mentoring and see it as a means to help people and organizations learn and grow. They see mentoring as a way of life.

When you look back at the hierarchy of mentoring, the second step or the next level is that of a Great Mentor. If you were a "mentor" and wanted to take your skill set to the next level you would be perceived to be a great mentor. I know that you are probably thinking, "who cares?" and in some cases you may be right. 95% of the interactions that I have with people are such that I am asked about my skill sets and how I became an internationally certified mentor. I have actually been interviewed by organizations and prospective clients to get an understanding of what I would bring to the table if they were to engage with me. As a great mentor I have invested some effort in improving my abilities as a mentor and have done some professional development to enhance what I already have for knowledge and abilities.

EXTRAORDINARY MENTOR

An extraordinary mentor is the one person that we all seek to become "our" mentor. They have embraced effective mentoring and the mentoring concepts as a way of life. They are typically someone that has had formal training and is certified as a competent mentor. They are Mentor Circle Facilitators. Their client base spans the corporate world, private sector, and entrepreneurial space. They demonstrate that industry knowledge is a "nice to have", not a "need to have", because they are comfortable working cross industry. They are humble and use storytelling/story-sharing as a means to share their experiences. They mentor in person and remotely using technology as a communication medium. They are a student of the mentoring process and strive to learn and grow as much as the people they are mentoring. They create that extraordinary mentoring experience.

Tomorrow you can look in the mirror while holding the descriptors for each of the hierarchy and ask yourself which one you most relate to. If you were to ask a friend, which term would they use to describe you? I tried this and was quite surprised when a few of my colleagues stated I most definitely am an extraordinary mentor.

When I think of this level of mentor, I equate it back to the book Good to Great by Jim Collins.21 The Extraordinary Mentor would be similar to the Level 1 leader in an organization. The Extraordinary Mentor would have great leadership skills just as the Level 1 leader would have great mentoring skills. What I have found the most important part is the quest for continued learning. The Extraordinary Mentor is always learning. After each mentoring session they use reflection and ask themselves three (3) questions: 1) what went well? 2) what didn't go well? and 3) what would you do differently next time? From this process you are continuously learning and enhancing the best practices of mentoring. The Extraordinary Mentor would be someone that would pursue a certification process as they see that as bringing additional credibility to themselves but also as a benefit to the people that they serve as a mentor.

No matter which path you follow your focus at all times needs to be on those that you are mentoring. You should be providing them with a deeper, richer mentoring experience will help them in whatever journey they are embarking on.

I answer a number of questions from the www.quora.com website regarding what we have just talked about. People are always asking how they can ensure they are picking the right person to mentor them and where they might find this elusive person. Finding the right mentor is important. That person needs to be a good fit for you. I recommend that you write down the attributes that you are looking for in your mentor and then have a conversation with your prospective mentor to better understand their approach and expectations. I won't engage as a mentor unless there is a commitment to the journey and that we have some commonalities that are important to both of us. Remember to take the time and to chose wisely as your mentor can help you with some life changing decisions. At the end of the journey, you will come to realize that you could not have made the journey on your own.

5. THE JOURNEY MENTOR

The Journey Mentor was created after a lot of research on the topic of mental health, mental well-being, Post Traumatic Stress (PTS), and Operational Stress Injury (OSI). What became evident from my research was that there was a much-needed place for mentoring as part of the support structure for the mental health space. My work with people who are suffering from any or all of these challenges helped me determine that there was a place for sharing the "gift of mentoring" and that it had a place as part of the support structure. There is very clearly a role for the Journey Mentor in the mental health space.

There is a role for the Journey Mentor in the certification of mentors. As perspective mentors go through the certification process, they can be guided by a Journey Mentor. A Journey Mentor can provide guidance on which path to follow and provide the support that is needed to accomplish the building of a portfolio as part of the certification process. The Journey Mentor is someone who has gone through the Certificate of Competence – Mentor and has been practicing mentoring for a period of time. The Journey Mentor would go through the Certificate of Competence – Journey Mentor and complete all the requirements of the certification process.

It is important to have experienced the certification process for the Certificate of Competence – Mentor and Journey Mentor in order to be able to guide others. The fact that both certifications are based on competence adds credibility to the certification, but more importantly, to the person who has been so designated. Understanding the case study process and the supplemental documentation as part of the portfolio package can be a little overwhelming for some. The Journey Mentor is there to alleviate some of that.

THE JOURNEY MENTOR AND MENTAL HEALTH

One of the things that became readily apparent to me was that people who are struggling with mental health, mental well-being, PTS, and OSI want someone who will be part of their healing journey. I am working with a few people right now and that is the message that I hear over and over again. Yes, they have access to professional counselors and psychiatrists, but they want more. They are searching for that person, a mentor, who will listen and hear their story, walk beside them, and be part of their healing journey and be non-judgmental. Those are some of the attributes that we would want our Journey Mentor to have.

As part of your mentoring tool kit you would have a resource list of people that you could refer the person that you are mentoring to depending on the modality that would best help with the healing. This may require the Journey Mentor to embark on some professional development to better understand what is available to assist with the healing.

WHAT DOES MENTORSHIP MEAN TO YOU?
BRITNEY'S STORY

In this section, Britney reflects on how mentoring and mental health can intersect, and the positive outcomes that can result.

Each individual will interpret the term mental health differently. For some it is not a term that individuals identify with personally. Instead, they identify mental health as something that other people experience. For myself, mental health is something that each individual possesses, like our physical health; each individual encompasses the aspect of mental health. Mental health has had a negative stigma associated to it, making individuals shy away from truly understanding and exploring their individual mental health. The more we explore the topic of mental health and are authentic in our individual experiences, the faster we continue to break down the negative stigma that is associated with it. In hopes of contributing to breaking down the negative barrier associated to mental health, I accepted the opportunity to speak to my own personal experience. In this chapter, I highlight three key components of understanding mental health that have been game-changers in my personal and professional life. I hope my knowledge and experience serves you well as an individual or within your experience in mentoring another individual.

SELF-REFLECTION

The first key component of understanding your mental health is the practice of self-reflection. As our mental health is intangible, it is important that we self-reflect on how we are feeling outside of our physical health. When we have an injury, it is easy to tell that our wound is not healing properly as the injury is tangible, we can see and feel it. Not only can we see when our physical health is off, but others around us can see as well. This is where the aspect of mental health becomes complicated. We cannot physically see or touch mental health; nor can those around us see a tangible representation of the state of our mental health. This is why self-reflection is so important. We must practice being mindful in reflecting on what our mental health looks like. Self-reflection can be as simple as answering the following prompts: How do I feel today? Do I feel overwhelmed? Am I tired? Do I feel like myself today? When it comes to mental health, it is important to recognize both good and bad days. When I speak to "good days", I mean those days you are feeling accomplished, the days where everything seem to run smoothly, where you feel authentically happy and joyful. When I speak to "bad days", I mean those days where you feel off, not quite yourself, where everything seems to go wrong and you find yourself overwhelmed. It is important to recognize both the good and the bad so you can reflect on common themes. What happens during the days I feel good? What happens during the days I feel bad? Can I control these aspects to ensure I have more good days than bad days? View self-reflection as your first tool in truly understanding your mental health, and own it.

YOUR ENVIRONMENT & DAILY ROUTINE

The second key component of understanding your mental health is understanding your environment and your daily routine. Remember when you were reflecting on both good and bad days and the commonalities that exist relative to your mental health? These commonalities can be directly linked to your environment and daily routines. When I speak to your environment, I want you to picture the physical spaces you are in: your office, your home, where you sleep. I want you to also think about the people who make up your environment, your family, your friends, your co-workers. In my opinion, your environment and daily habits have a direct correlation to your mental health; when you have those good and bad days think about your environment and your daily habits. Where were you? Who was there? What was the state of the environment? Was it loud or quiet? What were some of your habits that day? Did you eat well, get enough sleep?

For myself personally, when I have off days and feel overwhelmed, I immediately reflect on the state of my environment and my habits of that day. When I started practicing self-reflection and trying to identifying common themes that led to "bad days", I started to see patterns that I could control. I noticed I felt off and overwhelmed when my environment was cluttered and out of sorts. This directly impacted my mental health and would alter my mental state to feel overwhelmed. So I asked myself, is there something I can do to improve my mental health based on my environment? The answer was yes. I start and end my day in a clean space, whether it be my workspace or my home. Through practice and reflection, I learned my space can be messy and in disarray once I have begun my day, but it needs to start and end clean. Therefore, I adopted the practice that each time I end my work day or personal day that I tidy my space, so I can have a better start tomorrow and reduce the feeling of being overwhelmed.

Once I am done reflecting on my environment, I turn to my daily habits. I reflect on if I am getting enough rest, if I am exercising to de-stress and reset my body and mind. You will find your mental health is also correlated to your physical health. When you have healthy habits both physically and mentally you will see your overall clarity, happiness and energy levels increase. I know if I eat poorly (in excess amounts), do not get enough sleep, and do not get my body moving through regular exercise, it takes a toll on my mental health. I feel tired, irritable and foggy-not like myself. I know in order to set myself up for success for "good days", I need to have adequate rest, exercise and nutrition through healthy food consumption. For each person, your environment and daily habits will look different for you; that is why it is so important that you self-reflect on your individual needs, in order to fully understand your mental health as an individual.

FILLING YOUR CUP

The final key component to understanding your mental health is understanding what "fills up your cup". How do you mentally recharge as an individual? Just as mental health looks different for each individual, so too will the analogy of filling up your cup. This stage is really about understanding how the pieces come together for the bigger picture. When you think back to your self-reflection relative your environment, your daily habits and how it contributes to your overall mental health; what do you need as individual to fill your cup back up mentally? Do you feel like you are most energized when you are alone recharging? Do you feel like you get your energy from others? What do you need as individual to reset, mentally? In my opinion, we start and end with self-reflection when it comes to our mental health. We have to be accountable in understanding how the external factors of our environment and daily habits can impact the state of mental health and be vulnerable in seeking help if we need it, while also being supportive of others and their own individuality relative to their mental health.

CONCLUDING STATEMENTS

When it comes to mental health and mentoring, it is important to understand what mental health looks like to your mentee. What lens does your mentee view this subject matter in? What is their own personal viewpoint of their mental health and the concept of mental health? The answer to these questions becomes the foundation to your mentoring relationship. It is important that your mentee is open to self-reflection and being authentic with the current state of their mental health. Often as individuals we feel overwhelmed as we are seeking one solution for the scenarios we are faced with in life. If you are mentoring someone around the aspect of mental health, help break down the scenarios in their life through organic conversation. Breaking scenarios down and addressing them in chunks makes the scenario less overwhelming and can help someone reflect on the scenario from a different lens. Share your own experience on the struggles you have faced with your own mental health. Let your mentee know they are not alone and share your learnings that have come from own personal experience. As mental health is a complex topic that is often associated to a negative undertone, I believe it is crucial that the mentor breaks down these barriers to create a safe space for the mentee in terms of learning and growing. This happens organically when the mentor is authentic and vulnerable with their own personal experiences, as this lays the foundation of trust within the relationship.

SPIRITUAL MENTORING: DAWN'S STORY

One aspect of mentoring that can be particularly powerful and effective is spiritual mentoring. In this section, we'll return to Dawn, who explains how spiritual mentoring can help expand a person's perspective and give them a sense of deep connection to themselves and their world. Dawn writes:

Spiritual mentoring is the stuff that gives life deep meaning and purpose. Sometimes it is as straight forward as understanding the energetic exchange between two people and learning how to heal the intangible dynamic that flows between them. Other times, it encompasses the birth pains of a soul in the process of expanding. A common soul crisis, is when an individual begins to ask, "For what purpose was I born?" Existential questions like this can wreak havoc in a person's life, plunging them into darkness and despair. A wise mentor who recognizes this rite of passage is invaluable in helping someone having a soul crisis find the light again.

Spiritual mentoring is powerful because it breaks through entrenched human ideologies and offers a view from a higher altitude. Think of hiking up a mountain. When at the base of the mountain, a hiker sees what is in front of her—a tree, a stream, the trail before her. Half way up, the view has expanded and now the hiker can see a forest, a winding brook and a valley in the distance. The bigger picture can make all the difference.

Sometimes life's challenges are extremely difficult and there are no easy answers. Spiritual mentoring can be tremendously helpful to take a deep dive into the deeper meaning of life. I often joke that life always looks better when you remove your human glasses and put on your spiritual lenses instead.

For example, as a child I was a bit neglected. I spent copious amounts of time by myself with little more than my basic physical needs being tended to. For many years I struggled with bitterness until one day I realized that my upbringing was not my downfall, but rather, a great gift. When all of the other kids had pressures to get good grades and fit into the societal norms, nobody cared if I failed, nor did they bat an eye if I skipped class. I didn't have to worry about pleasing anyone or living up to someone else's expectations.

This gave me the opportunity to explore who I was and figure out what was important to me without anyone influencing my behavior. I was given the freedom to carve out who I wanted to be without being encumbered by someone else's moral code of conduct. Being allowed to live to the beat of my own drum meant that my creativity was never stifled. As a result, I've always excelled at coming up with out-of-the-box solutions to the most perplexing problems.

I'd been given a beautiful gift; however, I could not see it until I let go of the story that I'd been telling myself, that I had been abandoned and left without support. A higher altitude perspective allowed me to release the pain and bitterness of my past and feel gratitude for my challenging childhood. I would not be where I am today without those formative years of isolation and freedom.

It's extremely difficult to find our way out of the muck when we're so immersed in the pain that we can't stop focusing on the muck. Theresa always used to say, "If you're driving down the highway and you're focused on the ditch, where do you think you'll end up?" Her words still echo in my mind today, more than twenty years later, because of the profound impact she had on my life.

YOU ASK ME WHY I THINK MENTORING IS SO IMPORTANT TODAY?

We have a world that is filled with pain, stress and chaos. There isn't just a physical virus causing a global pandemic, but we're collectively experiencing a pandemic in the areas of mental health and spirituality at the same time. It's not surprising that one is mirroring the others.

It's necessary to deal with the mental and spiritual aspects of a person in order for that person to experience harmony in their life, and the same rules apply when we approach our current global affairs.

Let's face it, we don't make our best decisions when we're struggling with our mental wellness. This is especially true if we consider trauma recovery as an important part of mental wellness. I've had countless experiences where clients who seem to have it all together on the surface have underlying trauma that influences every aspect of their lives including their decision-making abilities. Most of these people have lived with the trauma for so long it's normal for them and they don't even realize that life could be better.

First responders will often tell me after a session that they didn't realize the call they've never forgotten was weighing on them like a ton of bricks. Not all trauma is obvious, like the trauma that occurs after an accident or act of violence. Trauma can also accumulate, for example, through little instances of chronic berating or criticism. Further, it can pass on genetically, through our family lines. Give me 100 people and I'd be hard pressed to find one without some sort of trauma. These people are every day folks who are bosses, parents, teachers, CEOs, and government leaders. They are making the decisions that impact others and our future.

Beyond our mental wellness, spiritual wellness is important too. People are far too disconnected from their inner guidance. Our hearts, minds and bodies are message centers that have lost communication with each other. Many people make decisions based on knee-jerk reactions to avoid discomfort, and they solve problems in ways that are familiar to them.

Thinking and doing things the same old way they've always done will produce the same old problems as a result. Whether you have a mess happening in your personal life, or a mess happening as a global community like we are seeing right now, we need a fresh perspective. It is imperative that we break through old paradigms, if we want to create a better future.

We are desperate for good quality mentors, at every level of society, who can help people access their innate wisdom. Whether it be the local grocery store clerk, a medical doctor or government official, we all need that trusted confidante to help us tap into our high-altitude wisdom and guidance. It's especially important in times of great stress, to dig deep into the depths of oneself, to be completely aware of why you're making the decisions you're making, because, if you're reacting out of pain, fear or old trauma, chances are you aren't making your best decisions.

There is great value in working from the inside out to achieve success in any area of one's life. Mentoring offers a powerful means of doing this, and the ripple effects reach far and wide, touching the lives of others in profound ways. Truly, the greatest gift we can ever give, is the gift of our own healing.

CASE STUDY #2

In this case study with one of my mentees, I show how mentoring becomes a relationship. It's not simply about one person's challenges, but about how two people with commonalities of experience can create a beneficial relationship in which both the mentor and the mentee grow and benefit.

Sarah was transitioning from a career of being of service to her country. She had engaged with a mentor to help her make that transition. Sarah had experienced some traumatic events during her time in the military which left her with having to deal with Post Traumatic Stress (PTS). She knew what some of her triggers were and had some coping strategies to deal with them. She was also seeing counselors and a psychiatrist. She was somewhat of an introvert. She had a number of challenges that we would have to address such as resume building, interview preparation, social interaction, identifying her triggers, and drawing support from her counselors and psychiatrist. She also needed help to make sure that she was being treated fairly by Veteran Affairs.

CASE STUDY #2 RESPONSE

My first sessions with Sarah were focused on developing a relationship and trust. We accomplished this by finding some commonality in order to build trust. Once the trust level had been established Sarah was more open in sharing some of her experiences and that she was dealing with PTS. One of the most important things that she reinforced was as a mentor to be able to listen and hear her story and what she is experiencing and to do so non-judgmentally. I wanted to make sure throughout the mentoring process that I respected those professionals that have been and who continue to provide her support as she continues her healing journey.

We worked on her being introverted and I had her try to meet at least one new person a week and to have a conversation with that person. She readily admitted that this was one of the most difficult things that she had to do. After meeting a few people and striking up a conversation she indicated that it seemed to get easier with each person and that she saw her confidence level grow with this exercise.

Another thing we talked about were the triggers that she needed to be aware of with her PTS. She was quite open in discussing the triggers and how her trauma had shaped those triggers. She was very aware of scenarios that she would be exposed to that may be a trigger for her PTS. She explained to me quite openly some of the trauma that she had witnessed and it helped me in being able to provide the support that she needed. As a mentor it is important that you can understand what your mentee has gone through. You may not be able to say "I can relate to that," as you may have never experienced anything like that. What you can do, however, is ask questions that will help you in understanding what they were and are experiencing. I have found that my genuine interest in my mentees' well-being helps to strengthen our relationship. This is an approach that I use with a large majority of my mentoring engagements.

CASE STUDY #3

In contrast to the previous case study, this example demonstrates that the mentor must be constantly aware of the possible pitfalls of the mentorship relationship. In this case, a mentee of mine began to display some troubling signs of dependency. Because of the trust relationship between us, it was my role to recognize those signs and take action.

Imagine that, as an effective mentor, you have been approached by an individual that you had offered to work with a while ago. She has come to you with the idea in mind that you would now be her mentor—or at least give it a try.

She advises that in addition to the mental health challenges that she has had she has just been diagnosed as bi-polar. She has also attempted suicide before and as she describes is a suicide survivor. Her family background is not quality and she seems to be one that is not a good judge of character and is a bit unsure of herself which then leads to some bad relationship issues. She was in a relationship with a much older man who was less than desirable and just not a good fit for her at all. It was almost as though she was searching for a father figure. A few sessions were conducted with her where additional information was gathered. She was very anxious for the first set of sessions and one had to pay attention when she was talking as she became more agitated when asked questions or asking her to explain outcomes.

It appeared that a dependency was beginning to develop by some of the statements she made. She made statements that she did not feel comfortable or safe unless she was in my company. These are definite red flags.

CASE STUDY #3 RESPONSE

The dependency aspect is something that mentors need to be mindful of. It can easily happen when you are working with someone who has low self-esteem or belittles their own abilities. They see others as always making fun of them and manipulating them to better their friendship with others. You see their anxiety level increasing as they talk. Any attempt to provide guidance is cast aside as they are the only person who understands. I had conversations at first where I tried to guide and found that all that did was to heighten her anxiety level and she would become verbally combative. Only she understood the situation and what needed to take place to resolve it. What I found that worked well was to not respond to her rants and by so doing I reduced her anxiety levels and she was more willing to have a two-way conversation. Perhaps that approach was another step closer to her becoming more dependent on me.

As an effective mentor working with people who are struggling with mental health challenges we need to be constantly listening and hearing and watching for the body language that would indicate that we need to probe deeper to find the root cause. In this person's situation the root cause came from her upbringing where I truly believe that she was the object of attention that went beyond your normal father-daughter relationship. She made reference to the fact that there was nothing like that that had taken place. That response came on its own without any prompting from me. I also observed her selection of intimate friends as one that would feed the need for a father figure. All the more reason as an effective mentor to be listening, hearing, and seeing any signs of the mentor fulfilling that father figure role. Your focus as the mentor needs to be going beyond this but you still need to be mindful of this situation as well.

The mentoring relationship is a two-way trusted relationship where the mentor and mentee both learn and grow on a personal and professional basis. A mentor is then someone that is relationship-based and trust-focused. For this reason, mentors must be aware of the potential for the abuse of trust, even if unintentional! Effective mentors can then diffuse and deflect the situation.

6. MENTORING IN THE WORKPLACE

Now that we have reviewed the history of mentorship, the current state of the field, and how mentorship can help people balance their lives, we can focus on how mentorship in the workplace can benefit both employers and employees.

My background is a blend of several different types of organizations. I worked for twenty-five years for the RCMP which included a leadership position in the RCMP. I've also worked in both the public sector (provincial government) and private sector with more than twenty-one years of experience. With the perspective that comes from such different organizations, I see no difference between federal, provincial, corporate, or private sectors, in the ways their employees are challenged to cope with mental health issues and post-traumatic stress. I have developed tools and gathered resources to mentor individuals to grow personally and professionally in positive and not so positive environments.

I love what I do, and as an internationally certified mentor, I work with people on a personal and professional basis and assist organizations to develop twenty-first century workplaces that meet the needs of the employees of each organization. It is important to me to make a difference, and I saw the greatest need to improve company culture. To this end, I developed programs and systems which ultimately increase productivity, lowers employee turnover, and supports the organization's growth. Seeing employee stresses increasing, especially with COVID-19, I recently created a safe space for employees (working and recently laid-off) who feel challenged.

Organizations today have neglected employees that are struggling with mental health, mental well-being, PTS and OSI. Some of employees are impacted by the environment that they work in while others have been impacted by an environment external to the workplace. This book would serve as a reference to those organizations. I hope that the stories and experiences I've shared will spur the desire for companies to set up this kind of support programs for their employees. To managers and HR practitioners, I would say that employees are your most valuable partner on your road to being successful. If we do not provide them with the opportunity to heal when they are struggling then we are letting them down and subjecting them to a life of pain and suffering—physically and mentally.

The benefits to an organization are that it has a deeper understanding of mentoring and what it can do for them and a deeper understanding of mental health, mental well-being and OSI. In today's workplace, being able to leverage effective mentoring is crucial in their ability to provide the support that they need for their employees. Mental health challenges are becoming more and more predominant than ever before.

I want us to consider "mentoring in the workplace" and mental health mentoring as different paths that we can follow. Let's look at workplace mentoring.

The first and most common one that you see is the implementation of a mentoring program within the organization. I know of some organizations that have built workplace mentoring into their organization's strategic plan. Some organizations market the fact that they have mentoring in place. They boast, "We support and maintain a mentoring culture!" Prospective employees, when asked why they applied to this position, often respond by stating that the organization has a mentoring program/mentoring culture in place.

This is typically driven by the Human Resources (HR) department at the request of the senior leaders in the organization. The objective of this program is the personal and professional development of its employees. This is done in some cases to create a mentoring culture within the organization, increase productivity, provide new and current leaders with tools that they need to lead others, or to help employees with their personal growth (self-confidence, self-esteem, self-worth, etc.). The program utilizes formal and informal mentoring relationships. Formal mentoring is done when the mentor program manager matches mentors and mentees together based on the data they have provided in response to questions in an application form. Some organizations will use a mentor software program that does the matching based on algorithms that have been per-determined by the software provider.

Informal mentoring happens naturally and mentors and mentees usually self-match based on some commonalities that they may share. There is also less structure around the relationship as mentoring happens when it needs to and when there is a reason to do so.

The ideal program is one that encompasses a blend of the two—formal and informal mentoring.

The second part of the journey from an organizational perspective is the use of effective mentoring as part of the support structure for mental health, mental well-being, PTS and

OSI. Most organizations do not have a program in place that addresses any form of support structure for mental health. My research has identified a place for mentoring to be part of that structure going forward. I believe that mentoring is a part of the solution to an increase in the resources needed to provide a path to healing for so many employees.

With all the challenges that employees are facing in the workplace and at home their well-being is being pushed to the limits. They are dealing with working from home, lack of social interaction, broken relationships—personal and professional, home schooling and remote working combined. Some have progressed to the stage of developing PTS as a result of all of the above.

Leaders in the organization see what is taking place but are not equipped to provide the support that is needed. Their approach is to ignore what they are seeing as if that means it isn't taking place. But if we are able to catch this in the early stages, we can provide the support needed to minimize the gravity of the situation. Ignoring and allowing it to grow can lead to a tragic outcome that no one wants.

What we need in the workplace are programs and resources in place to address the growing need. We need to put our employees first and provide them with the support structure that they need. This will result in the organization being more productive which in turn provides for an increase in the bottom line.

Leaders and co-workers need to be listening and hearing what their colleagues are saying. When someone says, "I'm experiencing this symptom and it is affecting my work as well as my home life," then we need to be in a position to respond to the cry for help and better yet to follow through on providing the support that is needed.

IS THIS ENOUGH THOUGH?

With increased numbers of mental health challenges organizations need to do something to increase the support programs, to increase the resources being offered, and to start listening and hearing for the signs and symptoms of someone crying for help.

The "gift of mentoring" is being under-utilized in organizations today. There is yet another role that mentoring can play and that is to be part of the organization's support structure for mental health, mental well-being, PTS and OSI. This likely sounds a bit repetitive but it needs to be heard. Mentoring when done in its purest sense is actually already a part of the structure needed to help people on the road to healing.

DOESN'T MAKE SENSE?

Think of the times as a mentor that you work with someone who has low self-esteem or lacks self-confidence. In either one of these scenarios the mental well-being of the person has been challenged and if not addressed could lead to a tragic outcome.

Based on my research, the numbers are increasing where people are struggling with mental health, mental well-being, PTS and OSI. It is startling the number of people that are fighting a battle that there doesn't appear to be a solution for or a willingness to provide a healing path to end the suffering.

Today most organizations do not have a support structure in place for their employees when it comes to mental health challenges. They may provide access to programs outside of the organization itself but they do not have an internal support structure which is very much needed.

Another thing for us to not lose sight of is the support that will be required to be provided to those that are care-givers dealing with employee's mental health issues. I know how important self-care is especially if you are wanting to be part of someone's healing journey.

I recently completed a workshop on suicide intervention that made it quite clear how important it is for you to practice self -care as much as you can. So, self-care no matter what we are doing is important. That makes sense.

Some key points that have surfaced in my research and from my practice of mentoring is that:

- Organizations should have a work place mentoring program in place
- Organizations must have a mental health support program in place
- Organizations need to have mentoring as part of the support structure
- Organizations need to invest in training to make sure that their mentors have the tools to be successful as what they do is life changing not only for others but for themselves as well
- Mentors are able to provide life changing guidance and must therefore have the knowledge and skills to do so

As you read this you are likely saying, "Well, what if we don't have any of these things in place?" The answer is simple, 1) without workplace mentoring in place your employees will not reach the full potential that they could, 2) without mental health support programs in place in the organization the employees will not reach the full potential that they could; sick time will increase; productivity will decline; outcomes will become more tragic over time, 3) mentoring is a key component in the organization's support structure and without it you are not realizing the full potential of mentoring in this capacity, 4) there is little sense in having your mentors work with people struggling with mental health issues if you have not provided them with the training they need, 5) having the knowledge and skills (part of the training) is critical as the mentors are providing life changing guidance.

If your organization does not have any of these programs in place then you need to turn to your Human Resources (HR) department. Have the discussion on how you can implement this in your organization. Sometimes we just need a little push to get things going. Take some of the benefits from reading this book and from your own experience based on what you are seeing taking place in the organization today. HR is the gatekeeper to getting things like this done. Sometimes though, they just need that extra encouragement to get things moving.

BUILDING ON THIS, A GUIDE FROM THE WORLD ECONOMIC FORUM HIGHLIGHTS STEPS ORGANIZATIONS CAN TAKE TO CREATE A HEALTHY WORKPLACE, INCLUDING:

Awareness of the workplace environment and how it can be adapted to promote better mental health for different employees; learning from the motivations of organizational leaders and employees who have taken action; not reinventing wheels by being aware of what other companies who have taken action have done; understanding the opportunities and needs of individual employees, in helping to develop better policies for workplace mental health; and awareness of sources of support and where people can find help.[20]

Mentoring is the difference and mentoring can be a part of the support structure. For this reason, it's important to remember that mentoring can be included as part of the solution! It's not only about career growth or meeting productivity metrics. It's about catching potential problems in the early stages. If employees are struggling with their well-being and PTS, then everyone from that individual through the entire organization benefits if they receive help before they get worse. The organization needs to make sure that they have programs and resources in place to address the growing need. This will result in the organization being more productive which in turn provides for an increase in the bottom line.

CASE STUDY #4

In this case study, we'll take a look at someone who needed support in the workplace, but who wasn't receiving it. His immediate supervisor was more of a hindrance than a source of solutions. Let's take a look at how to address that situation.

John worked in a large organization and is a high achiever in that organization. John reported to Melissa who had been John's supervisor for the last two years. During that time John had been belittled and chastised for a number of different things. It seemed that because of John's high work ethic that he was being singled out. John had taken the initiative to implement some changes that were operational in mind. He had discussed this with the employees who would be impacted and all were in favour. John did not discuss this with Melissa prior to implementation. After the implementation, Melissa severely chastised John via email and sent the message to far too many people. It was a public humiliation of John. John had to undo the changes that he made. Those same changes were eventually implemented by Melissa as though it were her idea. John has now become robotic and waits to be told what to do before doing anything. John's leadership has taken a severe hit. If you were the mentor in this situation, what would you do?

CASE STUDY #4 RESPONSE

John's mental health would be compromised in this situation and as a mentor I would want to be able to recognize that. I would work on discussing with people the power of effective communication and how he would have to understand the underlying cause for Melissa's behaviour. Melissa would not want to have it appear that someone had undermined her authority, hence the public humiliation that took place.

I have in situations like this in the past recommended either a Crucial Conversation workshop or a communication workshop that would help people better communicate their message. One of the techniques that I would use in this particular case study is the "pausing technique." One should always pause and think about what they are going to say and think about how it might be received. I always ask myself how would I feel if someone were to talk to me in this manner. If there are any red flags then you likely best not say it and you need to rephrase or reframe it and go through that process again. The more that we practice this technique the better that we get at doing it. What is also nice is that this is a skill that you can use in a number of different places. I had some employees working with me that had to meet with senior government officials on a regular basis. By practicing this technique, they became more adept at thinking on their feet and could respond to questions in a timely manner and with some degree of knowledge. Their mental health was not an issue.

What about the family? A person's family might be overlooked in this scenario, yet they will need to heal and being a part of the healing process as well.

We glossed over a key piece to the mental health and mentoring scenario and that is the role of the family in all of this. Family members need to be a part of your support structure and are a resilience factor that most always is over looked. In my situation the family was overlooked and they were left to resolve on their own. How unfair is that? In my situation my family gave up a lot of things to follow me all over our great country (Canada) and gave up a lot of the amenities that we now take for granted.

What was missing was a deeper understanding of the mental health space and the impact that it would have on the institution that we call "family". We couldn't do much for me but just maybe we could provide my family with the tools that they need to help me and hopefully understand what I was dealing with! By doing so I know that it would have made their life a whole lot easier and helped with moving me closer to the healing path.

Now if we could have a trained mentor enter into this story, we would indeed see things from a different light. That mentor would be able to provide the support required not only for the individual who is experiencing the mental health challenges but just as importantly for the family as well. The approach that we could use with the family is a "Mentoring Circle" which is a collaborative approach to healing. The mentor acts as a facilitator to guide a conversation between family members. Most of the answers to questions are already there they just need to be pulled from the emotions that surround these types of conversations.

MENTORING AND HR: MORGAN'S STORY

In this section, I asked Morgan, an HR practitioner, to speak to the company's perspective on mentoring. I asked for Morgan's insight regarding how issues such as mental health, mental well-being, PTS, and operational stress injury have impacted her role as an HR practitioner. Morgan says:

I think in this unusual year that we've just had in 2020 when a lot of things became everyone's problem, not just things that would normally be at home problems or personal problems, that would be spoken about and euphemisms at work or slang language or something. We've all just had to become a little bit more vulnerable and open with each other to get through this period of incredible stress, a lot of pressure and the most uncertainty, I think that our generation has experienced so far. So in the workplace context, I've actually seen some positive things coming from that because it forced us, at least from an organizational standpoint and an HR focus standpoint, is to refresh everybody's memories on all of the tools and resources and wellness, and mental health initiatives, and things that were already happening, and maybe weren't necessarily the priority that we should have been making them.

It forced us to start having those of conversations and be confronted with things in a more practical, real-world, okay, somebody is coming to me with this concern for their well-being and in the context of pandemic, that was not only their physical well-being , but also their mental well-being , because all of a sudden my colleagues and my friends that I worked with and people I supported in the organization I've been working for, had to become overnight, not only workers of our organization, but teachers and caregivers at home and perhaps the cooks in their houses for the first time. So the stress forced a lot of conversations right to the forefront, which in my mind is a good thing. I think it makes everybody more willing... When somebody comes forward and says something like, "I'm struggling," or, "I'm having a hard time," or alludes to something challenging in their life and names it and sort of brings it out in the open, it makes it okay for everybody else to do it.

So that's a very, very positive thing. It also, I think, added to everybody's plate of what they were thinking about and worrying about in the year. It went beyond the usual "how do I provide a good life for my family and build my career, and be a good corporate or global or community citizen?" Now there was a life and death mentality of things. So one of the other illustrations, and some of the conversations I had was this idea of scarcity and this real concern all of a sudden that there wasn't enough hand sanitizer or masks, or what have you to go around for people. So it almost heightened everybody's awareness of all of these topics. So it became more commonplace for somebody to come into my office and not just tell me that they were having a conflict with their colleague, or they didn't know how to approach a difficult conversation in the work context, now it came packaged with all of this other stuff.

That makes the job simultaneously better because you can talk about things and it's out in the open, but it also makes it a more difficult thing to unpack with people when they've got many stresses and things that they're worrying about. And often, those conversations don't happen instantly either, right? You have to build a lot of trust with people, for them to even want to come to you and talk about those things. When I found myself, specifically in 2020, a newcomer to an organization, in a totally different industry than I'd worked in before, in a different sort of cultural context, where it was very chain of command type of environment, and these people are walking in and saying, "I can't find childcare and I think my husband is upset with me." And it was just thing after thing.

So it made for really rich and interesting conversations with people that helped build relationships even faster perhaps than they normally would have, which again is, in my mind, a positive thing, when people can just get down to business with you and share and get to the root of what's bothering them, then the sooner you can help them. So those have been positive things, but this idea of a lot of problems and a lot of stresses combined with internal pressures and stresses, internal things like often people's mental health is the last thing that they care about and care for when they have so many other people relying on them and wanting their help with things, that I think that just again, forced the conversation and brought that stuff forward. And so, one of the tactics that I used regularly in those sorts of conversations was to recognize when people were in sort of that fight or flight moment in their lives, and they were really having a hard time even sort of rationally thinking things through, was just to sit down with them and make a list.

Just the very act of writing down all the things that were troubling them and worrying them and sort of getting to a point where they can name them, because when you name your foe, it's easier to figure out a plan to be able to attack it or disarm it, or whatever you have to do. So that was one of my favorite tactics and a good strategy. I find that when you have a lot of things on your mind, the act of writing them down and releasing them from your consciousness and putting them out there so that you can close the book and have a good night's sleep, hopefully get a bit of respite, it's just a good practice in general.

So one of my favorite tools connected to that is this concept of sort of thinking about all of the things that worry you and are concerning to you in terms of the whole world, right? There's so many things that we've learned in the year 2020 we truly don't have control over, health and safety being one of the most surprising ones, I think for most people to learn in 2020. I'm losing my mind, my track of mind here, I'm trying to describe to you this tool. Okay, sorry. Reset the answer on that one.

So once we identify the things that are worrying us, make the exhaustive list of all the things that are concerning us or worrying us that we're not sure how to deal with, then we can kind of close the book on that chapter and move on to the chapter of what can we do and what is possible, and what's within our span of control and within our realm. And so in the year 2020, for example, we learned how vital hand-washing was and how the simple act of doing something so basic that we've learned from childhood, it's a basic life skill that most people have really never thought about. That's one example of a small step that public health has told us over and over again in the year 2020, that we can protect ourselves and our families by doing.

Even such a simple example of that is a good starting off point for people to say, "Okay, what other activities and behaviors and things can I build into my day-to-day life and my own routines and habits, that are going to help me conquer that bigger list of things that I really can't control?" Because by giving ourselves the confidence, building the confidence in what we can do, and what's possible for us to do, it gives us that little modicum of sanity. It's a good place to start and it's really the only thing that you can do in a year when things are spiraling.

At this point, I asked Morgan to speak to the issue of discovering that someone needs help too late to intervene early. Morgan answers:

From an HR perspective, I think there's two answers to that. There's personally, what I can do as a colleague and a helper and a mentor and a guide? And then culturally, as an organization, what are some things we can do? So the span of influence that HR leaders typically have in the organization is to come up with all these wonderful and weird plans and programs and things that they think are going to help, hopefully with a measurement or a factor of success, when we're moving the needle on something specifically to help the business move forward.

In past organizations, a tool that I've really come to love is just the raising awareness of these types of things and starting conversations in a safe way when it is not threatening for people, and it's just something that we're all engaging in together. So that level set of, we're all going to use these words to describe our emotions, and it's going to be more than just mad, happy, and stressed. We're going to expand our vocabularies, using some tools and different programs to increase the awareness, to make it okay, and make it culturally okay in an organization to say, "I'm having an off day and I'm not really feeling myself today." And just that simple act makes it okay for people to get in touch with that range of other things they might be feeling and dealing with, without having to dip their toes into an uncomfortable place of actually sharing what those things are.

The first step is making it safe to have conversations, to express yourself in whatever words and whatever way makes it okay for you, and this is sort of a good first step for you. A lot of things that have come out lately through the Canadian Mental Health Association and various supporting sort of actors who've come up with great strategies and programs for workplaces that are low cost, they're not a long-term commitment, it's not even a lot of time commitment to get those sorts of things up and running off the ground, but it's the kind of thing that I would definitely advocate for any colleague who came to me and said, "We're not sure how to start or where to begin with this problem in the workplace." That's a very safe and easy first step to take. From there, then you can start to increase awareness with some of your leaders or other key grassroots people in the organization who are sort of informal leaders, with perhaps getting them some training around mental health, first aid and awareness.

There are other sorts of programs and services out there where you can begin to parachute in specialty skill sets to keep people who are either by title or by virtue of their position, or as from their status within their peer groups in the organization, connectors and people who can be an informal mentor to other people. Because I think the greatest thing you can do in an organization, in a group setting is to have lots of allies and to find lots of people who can help you with these things, because as soon as you put your job title on the outside of your door or on your desk, you there's a stigma associated with coming to HR

sometimes, right? And it means that there's trouble, or somebody has done something wrong or there's something to be
ashamed of.

So don't be the single solution. It's definitely something
that I learned in my career, we can't be the people to help and
fix things for everybody, we need a lot of people to help us with
that and to champion these sorts of projects and initiatives and
services among the staff. So that's a great thing to do too, find lots
of friends and to get them to buy into what your plan is as well.

From a personal standpoint, there are some characteris-
tics and some qualities that make you an approachable person,
a trustworthy person that people want to come to and feel comfortable and okay, and safe sharing their truth or opening up, or
lifting the veil, or whatever euphemism you want to use to sort
of start those conversations. I've worked in a number of organizations where interestingly; it was quite male dominated because
of the scientific or technical nature of the work. And so, I've sat
down with an awful lot of people who, from the moment they sat
in the chair, you could tell they were very uncomfortable with
somebody taking an interest in them as an individual and a human being, and wanting to know anything beyond what the work
context was, asking questions about their upbringing, their edu-
cation, and all of the things that brought them to this place, where
they are in their careers today.

And so I think having an empathetic listening year and
being very good and patient with people to give them the time
and the space to find their comfort level, some people will do it
and reach it more quickly than others, and some people, it sometimes takes a while, but during that relationship building and that
sort of level set with that person, you can begin to understand
and see some of their tells, some of the things that might tell you
when they're having a day or something's not quite right in their
life, that might be the invitation that you need as a third party or

an objective person to sort of come in and ask the question like, "Hey, is there something you want to talk about? Or we can explore it together because it looks like you're not quite yourself today."

That's a phrase that I love to use. It's very disarming. It's very easy to put people at ease when you point out that you've just noticed a small change in their behavior that doesn't seem like them, and it gives them the grace to say, "Yeah, I am having a hard day. I am mad, I'm upset, I'm stressed," and whatever that negative emotion is that I don't want to share at work, but it's the invitation for them to be able to sort of want to open up if they're in the head space to do that.

So one of the fantastic things I received in 2020 was a surprise training session at a former employer who said, "We've got this SafeTALK program that we'd like to send you on, by the way, we've signed you up and you're going next week." And I said, "Oh, SafeTALK, what is that? That sounds great." And then I learned that it was in fact the tools and sort of the foundational level of knowledge to be able to have conversations with people about suicide, which as an HR professional is not a topic that I by chance probably have not had to sort of deal with in the workplace yet, but of course, know of personal and social circumstances where that has been an issue and sort of periphery of my life.

So at first I was quite hesitant to get involved in this and was not necessarily all that open-minded, or open-hearted about investing in such a training or a session, but it actually turned out to be quite eye-opening and really a valuable skill set that I've now added to my list of... I'm certainly by no means an expert in any of these things, but at least I'm gaining enough knowledge and awareness of these various topics where I can start to be at least a good connector and a helper of resource retrieving, and finding people solutions for things that I certainly can't solve for them, but it helps to build the trust and the credibility of being an ally.

And so that was really great. I think it was almost like the universe speaking to me, "This is 2020, and you're going to have a whole bunch of uncomfortable conversations this year, and you don't even know it yet." This is actually pre-pandemic when I got to go on that course, and then of course, all of the social situations came up this year with the Black Lives Matter protests, a lot of anti-police sentiment and just some really startling social conversations that we've had this year, and has crept into the workplace through a number of channels. So this has been the supercharged year of all of the things and all of the feelings.

I asked Morgan whether she felt that organizations hadn't gone far enough yet in terms of establishing mental health supports in the workplace.

For my experience in the places that I've worked, I think, yes. I think we're doing a professional and surface level start. I think a lot of the activities and things that I've seen, the initiatives that I've personally been involved in or seen have been a good start, but I think the depth of this conversation in this area of knowledge, it's so new, right? Because for the last however many years that this has been a secret, or it's been something that people haven't talked about, we're still at the very early stages of change in this one. So there's lots more work to do. I think a lot of the people probably in the roles who have had to roll these things out too, aren't necessarily the right people to be designing all of these programs, right?

This is a much more personal style of program and service, it's a more empathetic and just in your face topic than most organizations and professional places prefer to keep it at arms length, and refer people to EAP services or other things that are quite well-intentioned, but maybe don't really honor the true connection that we have with our colleagues and with people that we have in some cases spent entire careers with, right? These are our friends too, they are not necessarily our personal chosen friends outside of work, but they're still our friends and people that we rely on and we count on and we also want to help.

So I think there's also sort of an interesting evolution going on in the workplace now with the different generations and the different expectations and attitudes towards work, I'm certainly meeting many more people who are entering the workplace now who are less afraid to talk about personal challenges and things that they've got going on, mainly I think because they've just never been in a workplace or they had to be silent about it or keep it to themselves. So I think that's a positive thing too, right? It is the more people, more voices, the more listening ears we have, the easier a lot of this stuff is going to become because it doesn't have to be the old way anymore.

My next question, obviously, was how the impact of COVID-19 will affect us. I asked Morgan what were some things that she sees that will definitely change for the good and what are some things that she wasn't too comfortable about, that may not be so good in 2021?

The genie has been let out of the bottle in a lot of cases, right? With social media, with people speaking up more frequently and perhaps sharing more than they ever used to about their own personal opinions about things. We certainly learn things about people that maybe we didn't necessarily know, and now that we know them, we can't un-know them. So that is going to make for an interesting sort of rebuilding. When you think about an organization as a team, and you think about sort of the stages of team development, I think the pandemic has really pushed the reset button on a lot of things, because it's accelerated the change of flexibility of work accommodations, it's accelerated technology, it's introduced a whole bunch of new policies and

programs and things that had to be sort of... They've been implemented in an interim basis, but there is going to be a lot of
support from lots of people who are going to want these things
to continue on.

So I think that makes it challenging and interesting to
keep moving forward. I don't think it necessarily makes it a negative thing, but then on the positive side of the ledger, I definitely
see a lot of these wins for employees in a very positive light. This
has been an interesting year where we've talked even more about
the pressures of male, female roles in the home of caregiving, of
whose careers have suffered now because of what's happened
with the pandemic, and how some people have had to sort of
take a step back, where others got to sort of search forward in
their careers. Those are all really positive things, and the more
data we have on those things, it's easier to action. So we have to
keep moving forward and keep thinking about all of these things
in the context of evolving the world of work and how we support
people.

The mission now, I think more than ever is how to set
up our organizations in a way that people can feel like whole
human beings when they come to work and not just a person
there to do a job, but they're honored and valued with the wisdom and the life experience, and all the things that make them
them when they come into the office. So it's an interesting, challenging problem. And my fear of course, is that other people
will, as they have throughout this entire year, continue to say,
"When things get back to normal. When things get back to normal." Friends, that's long gone. There is no such concept. The
goalpost, as we speak with our public health officers and things,
gets moved every couple of weeks as we go through these phases
and spikes and cases and things.

So I think the message of 2021 is just adaptability and
maybe letting go and perhaps mourning some of those things

that aren't going to return to normal, which of course has an effect on mental health as well, right? We measure a lot of our lives and traditions and past practices and safe ways that we've known for a long time to do things so that in itself is going to create more anxiety and more concern, and we're worried for a lot of people. So more tough conversations ahead, more beautiful opportunities to learn from each other and hear and understand different viewpoints. And hopefully, if we take one thing away from all of this, it is in fact that we are equally human and equally experiencing this strange period of time that we're in, and nobody really has the right answer.

A philosophy that I live by and practice personally and professionally a lot, and hadn't really until the last couple of years realized that I was truly doing it, is that value of listening more than you speak and being patient enough to ask as many questions as you need to, to really understand what's going on, on the other side of the table, rather than making assumptions or moving too quickly to a solution, for people who sometimes just aren't ready for that stage yet. So I would encourage as many people as possible to do as much listening as you can, as much walking the mile in the other person's shoes as you possibly can, because I think it's truly the antidote to misunderstandings and hurt feelings. It's certainly served me very well, it's also gotten me into trouble a time or two, but I think more often than not, it's added to my brand and my personal sort of ethos of, I'm not an expert in all of these things and I want to know as many other viewpoints and perspectives as I can.

MENTORING AND CHANGE MANAGEMENT: YVONNE'S STORY

I am truly fortunate, truly blessed to have Yvonne contribute to this book. We had a conversation about mentoring in the change management field, and how that intersects with mental health. Our conversation is included below.

When I think about change management and the impact of mentoring and the support that comes from mentoring in that environment, I go back to my last 10 years in corporate where my job was eliminated seven times. At the time, I really hadn't thought about how often that had happened until I left. I actually left the organization and went back and counted and what really stood out for me, from my own personal frame of reference, was the people that helped me through that journey. I'll take a moment here to talk about the role of coach, leader, manager and mentor. So in those situations, often the organization was changing from top to bottom, which meant that leaders, all the way along the way, your direct manager are often impacted by the same change that you, yourself were and the reality was they were impacted by it at a more senior level.

So not always, but often, the more senior the level, the more ego and sense of self is also wrapped up in the role. Those leaders' and managers' intent was to be supportive and to be kind and available and listening and welcome. But the truth was, they were dealing with all of those things themselves and often with nowhere to go because they themselves are considered to be the rock or the person who's supposed to guide the organization through this. So those folks who often also serve the role and function of coach or if you had an indirect leader who provided some of that coaching alignment with your organizational goals, they themselves also felt conflicted in their alignment to the organizational intent, whether it be streamlining, enhanced efficiencies, better clarity of roles, et cetera, versus what was really best for you as an individual and someone who was looking for guidance.

I'd like to say that this was more prevalent earlier in my career than later in my career, but that's not the case. I would say that every one of those changes that I went through both as a junior manager and all the way through to an executive, it was still the same situation where your coach, leader, managers were caught in the politics and in the organizational realities of those changes and had to balance as a result of that, their interest and guidance to myself. So enter the role of mentor and recently, I re-read an article about mentoring versus coaching.

One of the things that really stood out for me was the tenure of mentoring versus the tenure of coaching and the fact that these mentors in my career, in my life and my experience, had transcended a number of things changes and/or over time then, really, my go-to people that I knew I could speak with, who knew me well enough to be able to tease out and frame my goals and objectives in context of my whole self, who I was as a person, what I needed, what was important to me and my definitions of success and how that impacted my family, so were able to guide me through that thinking in context of their experience, but also in context of who I was.

So at the end of the day, if that meant, "Have you considered positions outside the organization?" That there was no vested interest for them in whether that was a good or bad question. It was a question that was genuinely framed in my interest. So through that journey of personal change, I started to really connect the dots between change management and the goal of mentoring. When we think about the impact of change, certainly, your leader has a key role to role model and to sponsor the change. But when people come to really make change at an individual level, at a, "Who can I trust to guide me through this nasty journey?" They turn to people that they consider mentors and they say, "I know this is what the organization would like me to do. I know this is what my leader believes I should do, but help me go through what you see, what you believe."

Then typically, through a response of guided self-discovery, in turn, then they would take me through that journey and learning of how I wanted to fit in, in context of those changes.

Those changes, now I've seen that play out as a change management practitioner and leverage that to the extent of not only getting the messaging coming from the formal parts of the organization, but also drawing on outside forces, mentoring type of forces, forces framed in the wholeness of the person in order to be able to support them on their change management journey.

WHAT HAPPENS TO THIS WHOLE PICTURE THAT YOU'VE PAINTED WHEN YOU THROW COVID INTO IT?

Every person goes through COVID changes in different ways, at different times with factors that are around them that are seen and unseen. One of the biggest challenges of the COVID impact is that a lot of it is not transparent. If we were in an environment, whether a social environment or a work environment, and we saw someone dressing a little differently, coming to work at a different time, shutting their office drawer a little harder than usual, eating by themselves in the lunchroom, maybe eating junk food if they're a health aficionado, we would respond to that. We'd say, "Hey, how you doing?" And would create an environment where psychological safety, where they could try to share or open up potentially, or if we know someone else has that kind of relationship with them, we might say, "Hey Doug, did you see Sally today, because she doesn't seem quite herself?"

In that journey and process, we would enable the people around us to be able to reach out or to find the connections that they need. One of the biggest challenges in the COVID environment is that lack of physical cues. It's really hard to know how people are feeling and not in a very Canadian way. You'll say, "How are you doing?" "Fine." "How are you?" "Fine." It's the opening to a conversation, but being able to take that moment to pause and say, "No, really. How are you doing and how can I help?" To the capacity and ability that each of us has our own reserves of capacity to support, then finding a way to do that. It certainly has impacted support mechanisms that people go through in change.

If I think about change management and some of the key drivers like coaching, communication, sponsorships or physical presence of the sponsor, training, those are key signals of how people are supported through change. Every one of those, of course, has had to change as a result of COVID. So not only are people personally experiencing the change differently, their support mechanisms are not in the same state to observe those changes. Then the mechanisms that are there to support them through that change are also all different. So it becomes layers of impact that, to some extent, we can't even know or understand how that might net out.

Let's look at this from the aspect of mentoring and mental health and change management. So when you look at those three, are there dependencies on each one of those with the others, or are they interchangeable? What your perspective on those three?

So I think they're definitely not interchangeable, but that's a great question because not unlike sometimes people will substitute the word change management for the word communication or for the word training, like all things change management are communication, or all things, communication are change management, that it's not true. So in those processes of connecting those pieces, there are aspects of interconnectivity for sure, but also, elements that need to be considered discreetly and independently. A client I've been supporting has been going through significant change at work, which has been exacerbated by impacts of COVID, so normal support environment's not there, so you have this impact of change.

You have an outreach of a mentoring support mechanism, but then you also could start to see signs of mental health challenges, where the edge of mentoring is no longer providing enough or the right kind of support to be able to tip them through the journey. It's harder to identify when you're doing mentoring only through a digital mechanism and when you're not as in as much proximity to them, but it does percolate up and what you normally might assess or determine through more than just dialogue, you actually have to bring to the basis of dialogue. So in a mentoring environment, if somebody was fidgeting excessively or kept looking at their watch or that you could see that there was some aspect of physical agitation, you would typically stop acknowledge it, address it, reframe and then determine, "Is now the right time or place to continue a mentoring conversation?"

When you're only approaching this from a digital perspective, their ability to fake it is a lot easier, quite frankly, because you're only getting those bits of percentages that you see through the screen. So if they're tapping their foot wildly, you're probably never going to know that or be able to address it. Those would be signals where if that can't be stopped, that's a signal of something more on the side of mental health versus something that is a natural outcome of change and that can be addressed in a mentoring relationship.

How can we deal with those challenges where the mentoring relationship can't be face-to-face? What are some of the things that you've seen that you do differently or that you do that allows you to continue with the mentoring process, albeit the fact that you can't do it face-to-face?

I would say I've learned, I forced myself to verbalize a lot more. If somebody is uncomfortable, often in a mentoring time, you'll let them stay in their uncomfortable space because that they're processing and internalizing. What I will do in this environment is be more explicit about it, "It appears to me that you're uncomfortable. Is that what I'm seeing or is it something else that the dog is barking and you can hear it off screen and that's got you a bit distracted?" So I'll try to frame what I might have been able to interpret in a physical space more explicitly through verbal interactions. I would say that I also am much more conscious of the duration of the discussions. So when you're in a physical environment, you can get a sense for when someone gets tired, because being mentored can be very exhausting.

You're thinking hard, you're searching your soul and your mind and your everything. So you can see, often, physically that fatigue, not in a bad way, in a good way, that you've stretched a good muscle, but you can see it in a physical environment. I feel, a lot more than a digital environment. So in the digital environment, I am aware of the time, so it's 10 minutes to the hour. This fellow has been in back-to-back meetings all day, has felt rushed getting to the discussion because when people end one meeting at 4:59 and the next one at 5:01, they're not really thinking about the physical transition, get a new file out, take a breath, get a coffee, go for a walk up and down the hall, whatever the case is. So I will often about, 10, seven minutes to the hour say, "Okay, is there anything else that you specifically wanted to cover today, otherwise, give you a few minutes back to go and have a breath or get a glass of water before your next video?"

Some of that physical duration is also, I think, very real that so many minutes digitally is very different than so many minutes with a physical capability and also adding some dynamic components to the discussion. So what do I need by that? That so much of the digital frame is, it's an on-screen time, but when you can pop the ear buds in and go for a walk with someone and just have the same kind of conversation without the eyeball-to-eyeball environment and maxed to a certain head screen that it feels, for some reason, even though you can't see their face, sometimes it can feel a little bit more natural. "Let's go for a walk around the block," and it just does feel like you're taking a walk and the talk and that can also be a way to still support the digital component, but do it in a way that can, sometimes, feel almost a little bit more natural.

Based on your experience in mentoring, change management and having to deal with COVID lately, what are some of your lived experiences that you've had that you would be willing to share on how you've seen mentoring as part of the support structure?

The number of people reaching out has been significantly higher. I've always been a very active mentor. Doug, you've known me for a lot of years, but the number of people reaching out and the nature of their outreach has been different. I wouldn't say mental health-oriented specifically, but perhaps, isolation-oriented or sight-oriented so that I used to be able to pop in an office with three of my peers and have that, "How are you doing? What do you think about this problem?" kind of a conversation and they don't have to access to that or it feels too formal to do it over a Zoom or even a phone call because that wasn't the nature of their original relationship, so I had a variety of folks reach out to me in that context.

I also have had people reach out to me who maybe had not realized how much learning they themselves were personally going through. They weren't feeling themselves and they didn't really know why they weren't feeling themselves because as far as they were concerned, nothing had really changed, right? But then when you start breaking it down and identifying the pieces of discomfort or the things that just don't feel like they were humming the way they used to, you identify aspects that were part of their normal mental health routines that they removed, but didn't even realize they had removed; listening to their favorite music on the go train, coming and going to work; their transitions in and out of work-to-family and family-to-work and even duration of focus. People with young kids have had, I don't want to call it interruptions because it's people living their lives, but living their lives in segments that are dictated sometimes by outside forces that they are not accustomed to in a work setting.

Stop and start, we know from the study of the brain and it's hard on the brain. It's this whole gearing up, gearing down, gearing up, gearing down. There's a reason that people love being in the zone and get so much achieved there and so that loss of ability to be in the zone because of life going on around them, but not realizing that, not really internalizing that's why, "I just bit the dogs head off when all he wanted was to go outside." So helping people think through what is different, being aware that it's different, and then being able to frame their choices or decisions or how they want to manage their environment as an outcome of that or accept that it's different, then go, "Oh, my gosh. Now I know why I felt that great because something had changed even though I was thinking nothing had."

DO YOU HAVE ANYTHING ELSE YOU WANTED TO ADD TO OUR CONVERSATION?

Earlier, we were talking about the idea of toxic handlers. There's a phrase called toxic handlers and my first exposure to this term, or this concept, came from being in reorgs and people who were responsible for those reorgs, being the shoemaker's children. So the shoemaker's children goes without shoes; the toxic handlers in an organization often centered in HR, not always, but are the ones that support and guide and take the organization through these significant changes and then at the end of it are like, "Oh, my gosh. How do I clean my own toxins out, because now I've carried all of this weight from the world around me?"

So one of the areas that I've reflected a lot on is for people who are those toxic habits handlers, is helping them know that what you're feeling is really real and significant and more significant than perhaps at any other time. The places that potentially you used to go to, to cleanse and to rejuvenate through that journey, maybe aren't there in the same way either. So this whole aspect of the toxic handler and whether it's the people I interact with, that I rely on for that function or the people that come to me that have turned to me for that function is trying to just be very aware of the boundaries and of the need for replenishment of energy and all of those things in order to be able to be the whole person that we choose to be.

The other part that I think that is really interesting right now is the introverts in my circle are, I would say, a little bit in their glory, right? So other than the Zoom call reality, which some of them do or don't get caught up in, the introverts, for the first time ever, I would say, in their careers actually can close the laptop, close the digital interference and just be themselves, in their heads, doing what it is that they do best and not be thought weird because they don't sit in the lunchroom with everyone else. So oddly enough, I had a bird's-eye view to these introverts in my circle and seeing them, in some cases, as a source of energy because they are in a different space because of their natural wiring and biases. So that's been an interesting discovery for me as well.

When I am mentoring people, because the journey is their own to take, I support them. I hand them a walking stick. I, maybe, give them a glass of water along the way, but it's their journey to take. It is really important for me that they have the energy to take those steps and to do the work that needs to happen in between the conversations. When people are tapped already and not understanding where their sources of energy come from, first of all, they might not understand it. So helping them understand it. So what does make you feel energized? What drains you? Et cetera, and then helping them frame their lives in that contest in a conscious way. I love the Johari window because it really helps people understand their view of self, the world's view of self and then, how those things combine.

Sometimes, people don't even know where they get their energy from because they've just intuitively included it in their normal daily routines. But when you have an external factor that is jamming up against your world and creating different, true teams, all of a sudden you might lose those and not really know that you've lost them. So understanding first, what is your source of energy, redefining your world to be able to capture that the best you can within the parameters that the world has set around you right now and then setting time aside to literally exercise and be in those times that do energize you, filling the cup, being conscious of filling the cop and holding it, like saying, "Gosh. I feel really, really energized right now. I feel awesome," and not being quite so eager to spend it right away, but just really holding it and being delighted with that moment while it's there.

DO YOU FEEL THAT WE WILL MAKE SUFFICIENT ENOUGH HEADWAY WITH THE WHOLE MENTAL HEALTH SPACE BY INTRODUCING MENTORING AS A COMPONENT OF MENTAL HEALTH?

I give mentoring as an important and missing piece of the mental health spectrum as is one piece. So there are aspects of physical fitness. There are aspects of just soul-based delight that's prayer or butterfly watching, whatever it is. There are aspects of intellectual honing that are also a part of mental health. In the spectrum, though, I do believe it's an emerging understanding of how it fits and why it fits. In many cases, I think, could be part of the glue that helps people keep those aspects of mental health intact.

When you reach a certain point of mental health strain, you go to a therapist and you have people who are trained in a different profession to be able to address that. But when you're in the median, the normal curve of mental health stressors, a mentor can serve many of those same opportunities to help someone re-establish balance. Not unlike you're in a car accident, you need a physiotherapist. You sprain your ankle; you need a good physical trainer. So, there's aspects of the gradients of support and I think mentoring has an underrepresented skill in that gradient us support and so definitely an area that I think will continue to grow.

7. MOVING FORWARD ON THE JOURNEY

The journey that I have been on has been one that has been filled with a lot of questions. Fortunately, there were a few answers along the way as well. I had some personal upsets with the passing of my wife Debra in February of this year. I realized that my bad behavior of years past was directly attributed to Post Traumatic Stress or PTS.

I also learned that I was one lucky guy to have a spouse and children who believed in me and that knew there was a better person inside that angry and abusive person.

I learned that the support structure for mental health, mental well-being, PTS and OSI was weak and that we needed to, better yet I needed to do something about that. It didn't have to be that way. If that was the case then what could I do to change that or at the very least improve what is there now.

I learned that most organizations do not have the proper support structure in place to pave the path to healing for their employees. That statement rang so true in my own situation. There was no support structure to deal with all that I had done or seen. There was no support structure for my family to be able to deal with me and in fact all that they had seen or experienced.

I learned that a lot of people that have come to me for help have not been able to secure that help anywhere. It has forced them to retreat and bury what they are feeling deep inside.

I learned that if you engage mentoring at the right time in the story that there are a number of benefits that can be realized. Helping someone using mentoring techniques and processes can create a path for them to return to work quicker and be that productive employee that the organization wants. A healthy and happy employee can translate into a reduced turn over rate, higher productivity, more engaged employees as just some of the benefits.

I learned that behind a lot of closet doors are human beings that are crying for help but afraid to open that door and reach out for help. They are afraid what society will label them as.

I learned that mental health is a silent pandemic with a horrible outcome if the support structure does not engage. I have lost too many wonderful people due to a faltering and failing support structure.

It doesn't have to be that bad. We can make a difference and change the gloomy outcome that is before us. Through having trained mentors, certified to work with people struggling with mental health issues we can provide that ear to listen and be heard. We can provide the support that is sadly missing today. We as mentors, are not there to prescribe or diagnose but to listen and hear and be that person that they can rely on. Someone that will ask questions and guide us on our path to healing.

You see, through all the research that I have done and from the practical application of proper mentoring tools and techniques I have determined without a doubt that mentoring can and will be part of the support structure for mental health. The Journey Mentor can and will make a difference.

All we need now is for you to open that closet door, reach out, ask for help and grab the hand that is offered. Your journey, your path to healing. begins now.

CITATIONS

1 "Mental Health and Substance Use." *World Health Organization,* June 2021.https://www.who.int/mental_health/prevention/suicide/suicideprevent/en/ Accessed June 26, 2021.

2 "The World Health Report 2001: Mental Health Disorders Affect One in Four People." *World Health Organization,* Sep 2001, https://www.who.int/whr/2001/media_centre/press_release/en/. Accessed June 26, 2021.

4 Post Traumatic Stress is referred to as PTSD, PTS, Post Traumatic Stress Disorder. There are enough stigmas attached to PTS that referring to it as a "Disorder" is not recommended.

5 "Post-Traumatic Stress Disorder (PTSD)." *Mayo Clinic,* Jul 2018, https://www.mayoclinic.org/diseases-conditions/post-traumatic-stress-disorder/symptoms-causes/syc-20355967. Accessed 28 Jun 2021.

10 "Operational Stress Injury (OSI)". *eMentalHealth,* May 2020, https://www.ementalhealth.ca/Ottawa-Carleton/Operational-Stress-Injury-OSI/index.php?m=article&ID=13254. Accessed June 28, 2021.

15,20 "Mental Health in the Workplace." World Health Organization, 2021, https://www.who.int/teams/mental-health-and-substance-use/mental-health-in-the-workplace. Accessed June 28, 2021.

3,6,7,9,11,12,13,16,17,18,19 *Ibid.*

21 Collins, Jeff. *Good To Great: Why Some Companies Make the Leap...And Others Don't.* HarperBusiness, 2001.

ABOUT THE AUTHOR

Doug Lawrence is an International Certified Mentor and holds two Mentor Certifications; Certificate of Competence – Mentor and the Certificate of Competence – Journey Mentor from the International Mentoring Community. Doug is the only one to hold the Certificate of Competence – Journey Mentor in the world today.

Doug served in the Royal Canadian Mounted Police (RCMP) for 25 years retiring in February of 1999 at the rank of Staff Sargent.

Doug has been involved in the certification of mentors since 2009 when he first partnered with an organization to provide mentor certification based on knowledge. Doug has now partnered with an expert in certification to provide a certification for mentors based on competence.

Doug is a volunteer mentor with the Sir Richard Branson Entrepreneur Program in the Caribbean and with the American Corporate Partners in the United States working with military personnel in their transition from military life to civilian life.

He also works with Futurpreneur in Canada to provide mentorship to entrepreneurs. His approach in all of these situations is to be mindful of their mental well-being and to work with them to find solutions that best suit their needs.

Doug's Practice of Mentoring continues to grow and has resulted in his accumulation of 2,200 hours of mentoring (in person and virtual), 235 hours of speaking opportunities and 672 hours teaching others how to effectively mentor. He is recognized as a thought leader in the mentoring space.

He has been working with researchers to examine the role of mentoring as a support for those struggling with Post Traumatic Stress Disorder (PTSD). His experience in law enforcement coupled with working with people as a mentor who are suffering from PTSD has afforded him a unique view of mentoring and PTSD. His personal story is one that is compelling, and it fuels his passion about wanting to help others.

Doug is a firm believer that mentoring begins with a person's personal growth thereby helping to remove any obstacles or barriers to their professional growth and career development. As Doug has found, some of those barriers can be mental health and mental well-being challenges.

"You are Not Alone" came from the all to often stigma of people being afraid to ask for help, afraid to step out of the closet and say, "I need help". Afraid to extend a hand to say, "its okay I will go with you on this journey."

"You are Not Alone" came from cry for help and increased anxiety and depression from having to wait far to long for treatment and to begin a healing journey.

This book provides a solution to that problem.